EXODUS

EXODUS

BW SMITH

Rev. date: 05/20/2021

To order additional copies of this book, contact:
Xlibris
844-714-8691
www.Xlibris.com
Orders@Xlibris.com
830111

CONTENTS

Preface...ix

Chapter 1   Why?... 1

Chapter 2   The Project 17

Chapter 3   Breath of Life 29

Chapter 4   The Truth Shall Set You Free!.................... 35

Chapter 5   What's Really Going On? 40

Chapter 6   You Take the High Road and I will
             Take the Low Road 43

Chapter 7   A Child Shall Lead Them 51

Chapter 8   Am I My Mother's Keeper? 58

Chapter 9   Chicago - Chicago.................................... 61

Chapter 10   Promise Keepers 65

Chapter 11   Reality Steps Into View 69

Chapter 12   The Chosen One...................................... 73

Chapter 13   Revelations 77

Chapter 14   The Meeting 79

Chapter 15   The Graduate 85

Chapter 16   When The Chickens Come
             Home To Roost 90

Chapter 17   Who Knew Why the Black Man Sang 92

Chapter 18   On That Great Gettin Up Morning 97

Chapter 19   Parting Is Such Sweet Sorrow 99

Chapter 20   Smooth Sailing from Now On 102

Chapter 21   Steady As She Goes 105

Chapter 22   A Long Time Coming 111

Chapter 23   Be Careful What You Ask For 114

Chapter 24   Hello – It's Me! 116

List of Citations 121

"We, as a people, will get to the promised land!"

Preface

The idea of writing this book came to me in the Summer of 2015. In the wake of the police killing of Michael Brown in Ferguson, Missouri, and the ensuing riots that followed caused me to reflect on the plight of Black people in America. So, I want to thank my husband Anthony L. Smith, my Brother David Handcock, my Nephew Duane Handcock, and Author Steven Ivory for helping me to bring this novel to fruition. Without their input, help, and encouragement, this project could not have been completed.

It seemed like a never-ending story, I mean, ever since the arrival of the first slaves on the shores of Virginia in 1619, the atrocities against us have never diminished. We have languished under the 21ST Century cruel lash of this slave-owner mentality culture that has ruthlessly raped and pillaged our black souls, day in and day out. Not unlike the 1800s, there are those who seek to breed us as if we were livestock to profit off the sale of our offspring in their prison industrial complex.

We, as a people, have fought in every conflict faced by this native land, even before this was a nation. It was not without the help of Black men and women that this land state became a nation, yet we have never partaken of full-fledged equal rights owed to all Americans. Although we as a people, have often been denied basic human rights inalienable to all human beings, yet we continue to help make this country, the greatest nation on the face of the earth.

After coming to the rescue of this Republic during the Civil War, we were rewarded for our efforts, the Emancipation proclamation, and a period in history known as "Reconstruction." However, both of these societal teases as they turned out to be, were short-lived. Reconstruction was set up to help black folks become self-sufficient as recently freed people. Poor Whites became jealous of the success of these newly freed blacks. So, the hard-won gains obtained by blacks through business, and politics were stolen away or destroyed. Freedom from slavery was also surgically extricated from us as a people through the Thirteenth Amendment of the U.S. Constitution.

Many people, and unfortunately too many black people, are not aware of the actual wording of the Thirteenth Amendment of the U.S. Constitution, Section 1 that states, "Neither slavery nor involuntary servitude, except as a punishment for crime whereof the party shall have been duly convicted, shall exist within the United States, or any place subject to their jurisdiction." Thus, the reason for over-policing of Black and Brown communities, but I digress!

As I was saying, with all the atrocities against Black folks in the news lately: Michael Brown, Breonna Taylor,

George Floyd... I started thinking. What would this country be like if all Black people decided that they had enough and were no longer going to put up with the ill-treatment in this country? What if we as a people, were to cash in our chips and leave this corrupt card game of a nation and go back to Africa. I was surprised to see the following CNN News report: "June 17, 2020: Ghana has a message for African Americans: Come home." I said, "Wow, this is more than just a novel; This is a clarion call!"

Chapter 1

WHY?

Jamille!? Jeremiah!? Hey – I need somebody to go to the store – we are out of eggs and OJ for breakfast tomorrow. Jeremiah answers "Mom – which one of us has to go?" I don't care which of you goes – as a matter of fact – why don't you both go? That way you will stay out of trouble! Sarah looks at her twin boys and smiles as she remembers the day, she brought them home. Doctors told her that she and Thomas would not be able to have any children. In her younger years, Sarah had developed endometriosis and had a lot of scar tissue, which resulted in her becoming infertile. So, everyone thought! One year and exactly two months after becoming husband and wife, Sarah was pregnant – WITH TWINS!!! She and Thomas were ecstatic!!!

When the twins were born, all the nurses on the floor said that the boys were sooo good and that they didn't cry much. I remember the head nurse coming into my room saying, "Mr. and Mrs. Harris have you come up with names for your twins yet?" Thomas and I were so surprised and happy about the pregnancy that we didn't think of names like most parents do when they are pregnant. We both poured over books and listened to suggestions from family and friends, but nothing hit home with us. We knew that we didn't want the average "twin" names – whatever they were. Thomas wanted them to have their own identity, and he wanted them to have strong names. We finally came up with Jamille (we liked the spelling) and Jeremiah (a Biblical name). Thomas was so proud, holding his two boys. He just kept looking at them and smiling as if to say, "these are my boys"!!! I DID THIS!!! Hahahaha yeah while I laid there exhausted as all get out! Of course – I had nothing to do with it!

Sarah is a freelance accountant and works out of their home. She homeschooled both her children for the first 5 years of their school life. She did not want anyone other than herself or her husband to influence their lives until they reached a certain age. An age where they would be able to ask questions about things they did not understand.

Sarah came from a family where both parents were present in the home. Her parent's marriage of 45 years was a testimony to how she wanted her marriage to be. Sarah's mom was a stay-at-home mom, and her dad was an educator. Before Sarah became a Harris, she was Sarah Ann Myers.

Her dad, Edwin Myers was the first black professor at the prestigious Austell Hall University in Arbor Michigan. It is no wonder that Sarah decided to go to an HBCU and chose Spelman in Atlanta, Georgia. At first, her parents were dead set against her going to school so far away from home, but Sarah was a determined woman (a trait she certainly inherited from her dad) and finally convinced her parents that it was where she wanted to go – and was going. That is where she met her future husband. Thomas was a student at Morehouse College in Atlanta.

Sarah and Thomas met at a rally that was being held on Spelman's campus. The rally was focused on immigration and how the Civil Rights Act of 1964 was being compromised. The two were chosen to be on a debate team, and they have been inseparable ever since. Upon graduation, Sarah and Thomas remained in Atlanta and lived together for one year (against both parent's wishes) before solidifying their union. Their marriage in May of 1999 was everything that Sarah wanted it to be. Here she was, marrying the perfect man for her – only she did not feel she was perfect for him because she was told that she would not be able to have any children. Even though Thomas constantly reassured her that he loved her and that they could adopt, Sarah felt like she had let Thomas down as a wife, as a woman. Well, the doctor's prognosis was proven wrong when in July of 2000, Sarah found herself pregnant with twin boys!

Jamille sauntered over toward his mother, "Aah mom I was in the middle of a great battle – HA YAH!!!" Jamille does a roundhouse kick over Jeremiah's head. Jeremiah ducks and grabs Jamille's leg and almost knocks over a lamp. Now see – I know your dad should have never bought you guys that doggone game. The twins have been studying martial arts since they were 5 years old and now, they are both black belts. They both enjoy games that have to do with technique and skill regarding martial arts. One game, in particular, was Samurai Warrior. The twins loved the competition-type battles that the game had to offer. Some of the techniques used in the game were remarkably similar to what they had been taught. I always thought those games were much too violent for 14-year-olds. Although, I must admit – you both are doing great in your martial arts classes. Just remember what your teacher told you about discipline and behavior – remember what he said – NOT IN THE HOUSE!!!! Both boys yell out "sorry mom."

Sarah gives Jamille the money. Now here's a 20 – it should be more than enough for eggs and OJ. Jamille – do NOT spend my change on candy! I don't know what I'm gonna do about that sweet tooth you have! On second thought – Jeremiah you hold the money. I know you won't spend your momma's change. Now go on before it gets too late – your father will be home soon and . . . . here he is now. As Thomas comes through the door, the boys are running past him. Hi, pop – hey pop!! Whoaaa where are yall going? Babe they're going to the store to get some eggs and OJ for our breakfast tomorrow. Thomas drops his briefcase and rubs his hands together saying "boy do I look forward to our weekends - ohhhh yeah – breakfast and then PJ's all day! Movie weekend!!! Thomas walks over to Sarah and gives her a big kiss.

Thomas Harris, Morehouse grad, is an investment broker for a prestigious real-estate consulting firm. He is one of four people of color on his job. He works hard and loves spending time with his family on the weekends. He makes sure that he is available for them, as his father was not around when he was growing up. Thomas is a very proud man who, with the help of his mother, put himself through college and made sure that he positioned himself to obtain a well-paying job. Thomas did not know his father and had no one but his mom to teach him the things that he should know about being a man. His mother made sure that he acquired a thirst for learning, was neat, and mannerable. She told him that those three things would take him far in this cold world. Hey babe! I'm starving – what's for dinner tonight?

Jeremiah, stop playing! Man, if you lose that money mom gave you, we are gonna be in a lot of trouble! Hiyahhh!!!! - Jeremiah kicks out at Jamille and then grabs him from behind. Jamille starts to laugh and does a move that gets him out of his brother's grip. Wow, nice Jamille!! I can never seem to get out of that hold easily - you have got to show me how to do that. Once inside the store, the boys continue to roughhouse a little more as they shop around for the items they came for.

The store is huge and carries everything from food to furniture. Jamille, let's go see if the new pieces are in for the Samurai game!!! Ok but we better hurry up and get back. You go check it out while I get the juice and eggs! Jeremiah finds the display and is mesmerized by the pieces that are offered. One of the pieces was a beautiful makeshift sword that looked very authentic.

Jeremiah picks up the sword and starts to do his martial arts movements. An elderly white woman notices Jeremiah with the sword and appears to be frightened. She looks around for a salesperson but does not see one, so she gets on her cell phone and dials 911 telling the police that there is a black male in the store wielding a sword. The police show up right away.

As Jamille is picking up the juice, he sees two officers running past him. Jamille says to himself - what in the world is going on now!? He comes out of the juice aisle and heads toward the toy department when he hears, POP POP POP POP POP POP 5- or 6-gun shots fired. People are screaming and running everywhere. Jamille sees his brother laying on the floor in a pool of blood still holding the toy sword. Jamille drops the items in his hands and runs to his brother. The police try to stop him, but he is too quick. An officer grabs him from behind and Jamille uses the move that he used on his brother and gets out of the officer's grip. He runs to his brother crying why!? What happened??! He was crying and holding his brother. Jeremiah looked at Jamille one last time and slowly closes his eyes.

The elderly woman starts apologizing saying she didn't know it was a toy - she didn't know it was a child - she seemed to be in a demented state. Jamille screams, "why did you have to kill him!!!???" The officers keep trying to get him away from his brother but Jamille would not budge. Someone says, "can't you see that they are twins!!?" Leave them alone!!! One of the customers recognizes the twins and makes a call. Oh my God - yes Thomas - you and Sarah need to get here right away!!!!!

When Thomas and Sarah arrive at the store there are people all around - news reporters are there and begin to stick microphones in their faces shouting, "are you the parents? How do you feel about your son's death?" Sarah begins to scream "death!? What do you mean ohhhh nooooo" - they both begin to run in the store - people shouting let them through - these are the parents, let them through!!! When Thomas and Sarah get to the scene Sarah begins to scream and cry shaking uncontrollably all the time running towards the twins, she begins holding her two children. Blood is all over them all. Thomas stands there looking around with tears streaming down his face shouting, "WHO DID THIS!!? WHY DID THIS HAPPEN!!?" The police begin to reach for their guns - Thomas says, "OH YOU'RE GONNA SHOOT ME TOO NOW!!?"

The chief of police tells Thomas to calm down and that this shooting was an accident. Thomas screams, "an accident? An accident!? My baby is laying there in a pool of blood and you tell me it was an accident!!?" The EMS worker is trying to talk to Thomas as the police chief whispers in Thomas's ear that if he doesn't calm down, this situation could turn into a riot. Thomas screams at the chief saying now you want some order!? Shoot first ask questions later? GET THE HELL OUT OF MY FACE!!!! Thomas is trying to cradle his entire family in his arms, but the coroner is there, and they have to allow them to remove the body. Thomas says Sarah - baby please - Jamille please - I need you to be strong and help me get your mom out of here!

The store manager has gotten a chair for the elderly woman that made the call. They ask her to please sit down and calm herself as she is crying uncontrollably and apologizing saying over and over that she didn't know it was a child - she didn't know it was a toy!

People were yelling obscenities and saying Trayvon Martin all over again - when is this gonna stop - Eric Garner - they've done it again - these kids live in the community they never did anything to anybody - these kids come from a good family - oh my God they've done it again - we are not gonna stand for this anymore - he was holding a toy - he is just a kid - that's his twin brother - wow he was only 14 - these kids never caused any trouble - I used to see them playing around here all the time - they were very close!

Jamille looks at his brother and kisses him on the forehead. He then looks at his dad, who is trying desperately to tie his dead son's shoestrings that have come loose in the altercation. Jamille wipes away the tears that are streaming down his face and gently pulls his mom's hands away from Jeremiah. She is rocking her child in her arms, crying, and praying. Come on mom - they are here to take Jeremiah away and we have to go. The coroner is waiting patiently - telling Thomas that he understands and for the family to take their time. Dad, we have to go. Thomas looks at his family - feeling helpless he starts to heave and sob heavily. Jamille seems to have doubled his age in the short time that all this has happened. For him - time has slowed down and people appear to be moving in slow motion, as if they are all in a movie with no sound.

Sheila, the friend that called Thomas and Sarah has offered to drive the family home - telling them not to worry about their car and that she will get help and come back for it later. Thomas, Sarah, and Jamille follow the friend to her car with no objections. News media is all around trying to get statements from the family and any witnesses. The family says nothing - they get into the friend's car and are slowly driven back to their home.

Sheila and her husband Greg Carter have been living next door to Sarah and Thomas for over 10 years. As she is driving them home, she reflects on their first meeting, and how her husband was so upset about "those" people moving in next to them. Greg is Georgia bred with deep old boy Klan associations - compliments of grandpa and other male relatives. Greg grew up listening to stories about the "old South" and how it used to be when "blacks knew their place." Sheila is a city girl, being born and raised in Hollis Queens, New York. Greg had just graduated from Columbia University School of Law – at the top of his class when he first met Sheila. His parents wondered why he wanted to go to school so far up north. Greg replied that he wanted to go to one of the best, and in his eyes, Columbia was it!

While attending a graduation celebration at a nearby club with some of his friends, Greg noticed this very pretty girl sitting alone having a drink. Instead of walking over to introduce himself, he just sat there and stared at her. Feeling a little uncomfortable after noticing this strange man staring at her, Sheila started gathering her things to leave. As she fished in her pocketbook to pay her bill, she heard someone saying to the bartender, "this is on me." Sheila said no – no please – you don't have to do this – I have money. Greg smiled at her saying "no one said you couldn't pay – I just want to pay it for you." Please – let me do this. After years of school, don't make me have to use my law degree to convince you and the bartender to let me pay! I'm good and you will never win. They both start to laugh. That was the beginning of their love affair.

Sheila was an RN at City Hospital in Queens but was in the city visiting a friend when she decided to stop and have a drink before she headed home on the subway. Greg would be in New York for about another month before he headed back to Georgia, and he spent most of that time with Sheila. Sheila fell in love with Greg's southern charm rather quickly despite their cultural differences – and when it was time for him to leave, she was heartbroken.

Greg made many trips back to New York to see Sheila, and it was during one of those trips when he proposed marriage. Greg told Sheila that he had joined a law firm in Georgia and that he intended to raise his family there. He did not want to put any pressure on her, but she had to know that Georgia is where he wanted to live. Sheila did not have to think too hard about Greg's proposal. She was living alone as she had lost her mom when she was 15, and her dad when she was 21. After marriage, Greg and Sheila bought a house on the outskirts of Metro Atlanta, in Cobb county. Sheila knew that with her being an RN, she would not have a problem getting a job. That was 17 years ago.

In that time, Sheila and Greg had a son, who is now 14-years old – the same age as Sarah and Thomas's two boys. Phillip was 3-years old when the Harris' moved in next door with their 3-year-old twins. She hates remembering how Greg behaved. All he kept saying was "nigger this and nigger that" and "why do they have to live here?" Sheila felt as if they had gone back in time. A time that she did not want to be a part of. Sheila had grown up in Queens, NY! She went to school with all types of people from many different nationalities. She found out that Greg's experience with diversity was very limited, and if it wasn't for him going to school in New York, he probably wouldn't have intermingled with other races at all. It is hard to believe, but up until the Harris' moving in, she hadn't come in contact with this side of Greg, and she did not like it at all.

As the years went by, and the boys started school, Sheila would see Sarah at PTA meetings, and they would exchange friendly nods. Sometimes, they would discuss issues that pertained to the school and how the children were impacted by what was going on. Sheila also knew that their sons had become friends. The kids could not understand why they couldn't visit each other. Sheila explained the situation to Sarah and Thomas, apologizing for her husband explaining it on his upbringing.

Around the time when the children were about 10 years old, Sheila found out that their son Phillip was being bullied in school. He would come home crying and scared not wanting her to tell his dad. Phillip did not want to disappoint his dad. He was a very timid young man – more like his mom. He wasn't much of a fighter. Phillip felt that his dad would be embarrassed that his son could not fight.

One day, Sheila and Greg both were summoned to come to the school, but when they got there, Sarah and Thomas were there also. Greg started yelling and demanding to know what had happened. He immediately thought that the twins had done something to their son! The boys were sitting in the principal's office, along with another child that was holding his arm as if it were broken, and the police were there also. Phillip had blood all over his shirt due to his nose bleeding. The police were there and had to calm Greg down because he kept yelling obscenities at the twins. Thomas started yelling back and threatening to do bodily harm to Greg.

It seems that the same bully had started a fight with Phillip – punching him in the nose. The twins came to Phillip's rescue. No one at the school knew that the twins were taking martial arts lessons – it was part of their disciplinary training. They were to be humble about their knowledge of the arts, but when they saw what was happening to their friend, they attacked the bully and wound up breaking his arm.

When Greg heard that story – his whole demeanor toward the Harris' changed. The parents of the bully came in and demanded that the twins be taken to jail. Greg stepped in and said, "I am the attorney for the twins – let's talk about this and see if we can get this resolved without anybody going to jail." Greg informed the parents that it was their son that assaulted his son and that he had been bullying him for quite some time. Greg also informed them that he could press charges and have their son sent to a detention facility (exaggerating a little).

From that point on, Greg and Thomas became the best of friends. Sheila and Greg knew that their son was a little different from the other children and was very thankful that the twins had befriended him. They loved their son immensely. Sheila made a sigh of relief as she could now be open about her friendship with Sarah, and the boy's friendship (as well as their parents) blossomed into a brotherly love for each other.

As Sheila pulled up to Thomas and Sarah's home no one moved. Sheila noticed that Greg and Phillip were home - she had called Greg from the store and told him what happened. When she pulled up, they both came running to the car. Greg opened the door on Sarah's side and tried to help her out of the car. Thomas got out and tried to help also – Sarah was still crying intensely. Both men helped Sarah into the house with Sheila following. When Jamille got out of the car - Phillip was standing there. Jamille noticed that Phillip had something in his hand. With tears streaming down his face Phillip held up a picture of himself with the twins. Jamille started crying and sat down on the curb, and Phillip sat next to him not saying a word.

The next few days were like a blur to the Harris family as they prepared for their son's funeral. They were receiving all kinds of correspondence from people they did not know – some were condolences, and some were regarding police brutality and how they should sue the police department. Civil rights leaders were calling and asking if the family wanted to seek justice for the senseless murder of their son. News reporters camped outside of their home for days. Jeremiah's schoolmates held a candlelight vigil on the lawn of the Harris' home the night before the funeral. The family also received a phone call from the President giving his condolences.

On the day of the funeral, it was pouring down raining. Jamille watched as his mom was trying desperately to get a pin on the lapel of her jacket – her hands were trembling so much that she could not do it. Jamille said mom let me do that for you. As he fixed the pin on his mom's jacket, he told her that he read somewhere that when someone dies, and it rains, the rain is washing their footprints from the earth. Jamille said mom – Jeremiah's footprints may be washed away but I will never forget him! Sarah looked at Jamille and said that's right baby – we will never forget our love. Sarah looked at her child and hugged him until Thomas told them it was time to go.

The funeral was beautiful. Brian Kennedy, a well-known Black activist flew in from New York to give the eulogy. As Brian spoke, Jamille wondered how somebody that didn't even know his brother could give the eulogy.

The days and months following Jeremiah's death were long and sorrowful. The activist from New York assisted Thomas and Sarah with filing a lawsuit against the police department. Greg asked if he could head up the legal team to help put the police officer behind bars – or, at the least, get him fired from the police department. As with most of the wrongful death cases involving police and citizens, the police officer did not lose his job, and he did not go to prison. The police officer was found to have acted appropriately, and that his actions were in line with the duties of his job. He was suspended – with pay for the entire time of the trial. Once the verdict was in, he went right back to work.

For Sarah – she was glad that it was over because nothing could bring her son back, and for her, everything else was just a waste of time. Jamille noticed that his mother, who at one time, was up and full of energy - lately, seemed to be a little out of it. What Jamille did not know was that his mother was battling depression. Thomas was angry most of the time – coming home yelling at Sarah for not doing something around the house. Jamille did not know what was going on with his family but he knew that whatever was wrong had to do with Jeremiah's death. He longed for the days when they were all a family. Jamille found himself being angry also and losing respect for authority figures. Jamille prayed that his mother and father would not give up and separate. He was so fearful of those thoughts, but he would not dare voice it to anybody. Those thoughts stayed bottled up inside of him for fear if he said them out loud it just might happen.

One day, while sitting outside, Phillip came over to see if Jamille wanted to go over some martial arts moves. Before Jeremiah's death, the twins had begun to show Phillip some moves to help protect himself against bullies like the one that attacked him in school a few years ago. Jamille told Phillip that he didn't feel like it right now and to maybe come back later. Phillip sat down next to Jamille and said, "I know that you are missing your brother… I miss him too. But I want you to know that you still have a brother Jamille – I will always be here for you!" Jamille looked at Phillip, and through his tears said, "thank you, man." Phillip said, "I know you don't want me to hug you, but we hug at my house so get ready – here it comes – I'm gonna hug you!" With that Phillip reached out to hug Jamille and they both started laughing – Jamille said, "no man - get out of here" playfully pushing Phillip away - but he allowed the hug anyway while the both of them kept laughing. Phillip said, "I love you man" – Jamille said, "I love you too brother."

Chapter 2

THE PROJECT

Three years have passed since that dreadful day, and Jamille is now a senior in high school. Sarah, Thomas, and Jamille had to get counseling to deal with Jeremiah's death. The counseling helped to keep their family together. Things had gotten really bad with Thomas moving out for a couple of months. Although Jamille was fearful of that happening, the separation did some good. Along with the counseling and separation, Sarah and Thomas realized how much they loved and needed each other. They also realized how much of a toll the situation had taken on Jamille and that they needed to be a family again.

In the years leading up to his senior year, Jamille had taken a great interest in Brian Kennedy – the activist that gave the eulogy at Jeremiah's funeral, and had begun communicating with him continually.

Brian said that Jamille reminded him of himself when he was that age. Jamille asked Brian the question that he asked himself at his brother's funeral. How can someone that doesn't even know his brother give the eulogy for him? Brian told him that throughout his entire life, he was devoted to civil rights. It was his calling. He told Jamille that he had seen a lot of injustices and some that were taken out on him. I have been arrested on numerous occasions; I have buried a number of my friends in the name of injustice. I have walked with Kings and broke bread with Presidents. I think that – no – I have EARNED the right to give the eulogy for a fallen angel. Jamille – I see that you have that calling also. Unfortunately, it took the death of your brother to bring this out in you, but I see it in you. I see it in the questions that you ask. I see it in how the last three years you communicated with me about the wrongs you have tried to right in your own community. You established a neighborhood watch. You made sure that everyone in your community had some type of recording device. You submitted a grant and received monies to buy these devices for anyone that needed one in your community. Jamille – you even created a youth movement organization dedicated to Black Lives Matter! I'm proud of you son!

It meant a lot to hear Brian say that he was proud of him and what he was doing. Thomas and Sarah were proud of him too, yet they were also worried about Jamille because he was always in his room reading, or on the computer. They were afraid that he was becoming introverted and hoped that he was not in his room plotting to shoot up someplace or something crazy like that.

Ever since the murder of his twin brother, Jamille had become very interested in civil rights, and the youth movement that he organized as a subdivision of Black

Lives Matter. He found himself always having to defend what he was fighting for – or against. He would say, "most people are good people. My intentions aren't to insult white people, but the facts are the facts. It's a fact that 9/10th of the global population are people of color, and only 1/10th of the global population is white, yet we are being treated like we don't matter. Yes – it's true that ALL lives matter, but right now – black people are getting the real short end of the stick!" With the help of his friend Phillip, they solicited everyone in the neighborhood, including all their friends on their social media platform to sign a petition to get a neighborhood watch going. Jamille made Phillip the captain. He got names from people that didn't even live in his neighborhood, but because they sympathized with him and his family, they signed. There wasn't that much crime in his neighborhood but after the organization of the Watch, it brought the number of mishaps to virtually none. Jamille was getting recognition as a leader in his community, a go-getter. He was very determined to not let what happened to his brother happen to anyone else – not just in his community but also within the country.

Communication with Brian Kennedy led him to become affiliated with the organization Black Lives Matter and helped with starting his own chapter. While gathering information on the organization, Jamille found out that every 28 hours, a black man, woman, or child is murdered by some form of law enforcement. Jamille found himself to be engulfed with the issues concerning senseless killings like that of Trayvon Martin in Florida. Trayvon Martin was a young black man who was gunned down in Sanford,

Florida by a neighborhood watchman that was not appointed by anyone in that neighborhood.

Michael Brown was another young man from Ferguson Missouri who was on his way to college a few days before he was shot and killed by a police officer who was just "doing his duty." These killings and many others were brought home when Jamille tragically lost his brother to the same type of violence. He knew that he would do something to make sure that his brother did not die in vain.

Jamille was so concerned with what was going on and wanted to help in some way that Brian Kennedy became somewhat of a mentor to him. Brian invited Jamille to New York on one of his summer breaks. With permission from his parents, Jamille met with Brian and got the history lesson of his life. A history lesson that he had never read about in the books he had in his school. Brian took Jamille to the site of the Audubon Ballroom where Malcolm X was killed. The site is currently the Audubon Business and Technology Center and the Shabazz Center. Brian gave Jamille a myriad of books to read and answered all of his questions. Brian told Jamille all about Marcus Garvey and the Universal Negro Improvement Association (UNIA). The UNIA was proclaimed to be the largest mass movement in Black American history with a "back to Africa" message. Brian was filled with a wealth of knowledge and he shared it all with Jamille.

Brian told Jamille that he had walked with Kings. Jamille was not surprised to learn that Brian had marched with Martin Luther King and went to jail on numerous occasions. Brian told him that he cannot be afraid. If you talk the talk, you have to walk the walk. He told Brian about the incident that happened on the Edmund Pettus Bridge. The bridge is named after a U.S. Senator from Alabama, who was also a Grand Dragon of the Alabama Ku Klux Klan. That bridge was the site of a conflict that has gone down in history as Bloody Sunday.

On that Sunday, March 7, 1965, armed policemen attacked Civil Rights Leader, John Lewis and peaceful demonstrators with billy clubs and tear gas as they were trying to march to the Alabama state capitol, Montgomery. Brian was there, along with other civil rights leaders. On March 11, 2013, the bridge was declared a National Historic Landmark. Jamille told Brian that he doesn't quite understand why anyone would want to make something like that, where a tragedy happened, into a national landmark? Brian told Jamille that one should never forget their past lest they be doomed to repeat it. Maybe honoring these places and things may not seem appropriate but it keeps it, or them out in the forefront never to be forgotten.

By the time Jamille's vacation was over, he was a different person. He was more aware of the world and his surroundings and seemed much wiser than other children of his age. He had so many questions and he was very grateful to Brian for spending time with him and teaching him about a history that showed no face in the teachings he had gotten in his school.

Brian told him about all the inventions that Black people contributed to this country. Inventions like blood banks, the refrigerator, the electric trolley, the dustpan, comb, mop, brush, clothes dryer, lawnmower, traffic signals, the pen and pencil sharpener; and from people like Otis Boykin, who invented the artificial heart pacemaker control unit; Henry Brown, the modern-day fireproof safe; Granville T. Woods, the multiplex telegraph; here's one he was sure his brother Jeremiah would have liked – Gerald A. Lawson, the modern home-video gaming console; Patricia Bath, the cataract laser phaco probe; Marc Hannah, 3-D graphics technology that is used in films; and Garrett Morgan, the modern-day gas mask.

On Jamille's last day in New York, Brian took Jamille to the site where the 911 terrorist attacks had taken place. His parents had told him and his brother about what happened, but to see the site was truly surreal. Jamille was overcome with emotion. Brian told Jamille that when this tragedy took place, American people seemed they had forgotten their differences and for a brief moment - all lives did matter.

Yes - when Jamille got back to Atlanta, he stayed in his room a lot and read all the books Brian had given him. He knew that his parents were concerned about what he was doing. Phillip was the only person that he had divulged his plans to. As a pre-requisite to graduating from high school, all seniors had to submit a thesis paper on any subject of their choosing. Armed with his communications with Brian, and the summer that he spent with him in New York, Jamille knew exactly what he wanted to write about.

It's Saturday morning. Thomas woke up to the smell of bacon frying. He couldn't help but think about how good Sarah takes care of him and Jamille. He thinks about how hard she took the death of their son, and how he almost lost her - once by leaving her, and once, because of her depression. They all had taken it so hard and dealt with it in their own ways. Thank God they made it through and back to each other.

Saturdays were always dedicated to a big breakfast, pajamas all day, and movies – movies - movies. After working all week, Thomas looked forward to these Saturdays with his family.

Jamille!!! Get up man – don't you smell that bacon!!? Jamille laughs out loud – dad I'm way ahead of you (coming out of the room in his pajamas). They both start for the steps and then start running to see who could get down the steps faster.

Sarah hears the noise and tells them to stop running – you know your father is too old to be trying to run down those stairs! There was a knock on the back door before Thomas can give a rebuttal to Sarah's remark, Thomas looks through the curtain and sees Greg, Sheila, and Phillip in their pajamas. Come on in – you are just in time. Honey – we have guests for pajama day. Sarah tells them all to sit down because breakfast is served! Sheila is laughing so hard telling everybody how they had to sneak across the lawn in their pajamas without anybody seeing them.

What a spread – bacon, eggs, sausages, biscuits, grits, and OJ. Thomas asks Phillip to please say grace and when he was done, everybody dug in.

Sheila tells Sarah that breakfast was great and offers to help with clearing off the table and cleaning the dishes. Thomas tells all the guys to come on in the living room and leave the cleaning to the women. Everybody starts to laugh. Thomas and Greg take their coffee with them.

Greg and Sheila both thank Sarah for the meal and ask, "what's on the movie agenda for today?" Jamille and Phillip are looking through the cabinet for some movies. Thomas says that the youngsters are picking out some movies. Let's see what they come up with.

Thomas and Greg go out on the patio to drink their coffee. Greg looks at their boys and says – you know Thomas – look at them – they are both 17 now – seniors in high school. We raised them right. They could be anywhere, but they are here with us on a Saturday – in their pajamas – about to watch movies with their families.

Yeah, I know man – they could be anywhere else. Listen, Greg, – I wanted to ask you something. Has Phillip been saying anything to you about this organization that Jamille started? I mean – is he a part of it?

Well, I don't know if Phillip is a part of it because it has something to do with people of color and the injustices that they face here in America. Well, I take that back, knowing Phillip the way that I do – he probably is. I never asked him.

Would you be offended if he were Greg? No Thomas – I would be proud that my son was standing up for something he believed in. I wouldn't want him to get hurt in any way; nevertheless, I would be proud. Why do you ask?

Jamille has been doing a lot of reading. I saw some of the books and they were on the rise and fall of the Black Panther movement, Marcus Garvey, Gandhi, Malcolm X, MLK. He has also been communicating with Brian Kennedy throughout the years. Brian even invited Jamille to come to New York as his guest. Sarah and I gave him our permission this summer and he went for two weeks. You know Brian helped him to get funding for those recording devices. I don't know what to make of it. It seems my son has turned into an activist of some sort.

Are you worried Thomas? I don't know – should I be Greg? I mean – you are the lawyer – what do you make of it? I'm a lawyer – not a detective man. Why don't you just ask him what he is up to? I don't want him to think that I'm snooping around in his things. Yet – that is exactly what you are doing. The two men look at each other – take a sip of their coffee and go back into the living room. Ok – Thomas rubs his hands together – what did you guys pick out? Well, dad – we picked out an oldie but goodie – we picked The Clash of the Titans.

Sarah says, "Wow I love Greek mythology"! Sheila says "ok – I can watch that – it's been a long time!" Phillip says, "cool – they did a remake of this, but I want to see this one – it's the original!" Greg says, "alright start er up!!"

In bed on Sunday night – Sarah lets out a big sigh. Thomas asks, "What's on your mind babe?" Thomas – I was wondering about how many more pajama Saturdays are we going to have with Jamille. He will be graduating this year, and then he will be going off to college. I'm going to miss him so much! Sarah – you knew he had to grow up sometime. Thomas smiles and puts his arms around Sarah. Hell – I'm gonna miss him too – especially when I think about our pajama Saturdays. Listen – you and I can still do pajama Saturdays – and it will be a lot more fun here by ourselves. We can do – NO PAJAMA Saturdays!!!

Sarah takes her pillow and hits Thomas – they laugh – look at each other – then Sarah just lays her head in Thomas' chest. They both lay there not saying a word – just holding each other.

Monday – Jamille comes running into the house – mom – where's dad? What's going on Jamille? Your dad should be home soon – what's wrong? Mom – I turned in my idea for my senior project assignment today and I want to talk it over with the both of you. I am so excited!!

When Thomas gets home – Jamille asks him to come into the living room. Thomas wants to know what all the excitement is about. Sarah says, "he wants to talk to the both of us about his senior school project."

Mom – dad – these last few years since Jeremiah's death, have been hard. I have been watching news story after news story about injustices done to our people. It has gotten so that Black people can't even go for a Sunday drive or walk in the park without being harassed. So, I got to thinking about a solution. I concluded that we are not wanted here, and I do not understand why we keep trying to live amongst people that do not want us here.

I have a hypothetical question to ask you. What would happen if every black person in America were to leave? Thomas says, "and go where?" Sarah looks perplexed – yes baby – go where? LEAVE – leave the United States to go live on their own island! What do you think would happen to the U.S. if that were to happen?

Thomas says, "first of all – an island would be too small for all the Black people in America." Dad – this is just a hypothetical situation – work with me. We will use an island for now. See – this is what I am going to do my senior project on. There are some 43 million Black people in the United States. I did research and found that we will have spent 1.1 trillion dollars in America by the end of the year. Imagine if all that revenue was taken away? The United States would collapse. Thomas and Sarah look at each other. Sarah says – Thomas - Jamille has lost his mind! Thomas touches Sarah's arm and says, "wait, babe – let's hear him out."

Mom – dad – it's all hypothetical. My teacher says it is a great idea for a project. Well – I just wanted to share it with you and tell you dad that this is what I have been reading all those books for. Yes – Phillip told me that you asked about why I was doing all that reading. I have had this question in my head for a long time – well since we lost Jeremiah. I was so angry and wished that I could have done something.

At first, I wanted to hurt someone – kill someone like they killed him. Then I got to thinking that I just wanted to leave. I started reading about the Black Panther movement and how they took control of their communities until the federal government stepped in and disrupted everything.

Next, I studied Marcus Garvey and how he wanted Black people to return to their ancestral lands. We live in fear here. This is what Marcus Garvey had to say about fear (Jamille pulls a piece of paper from his bag and reads) "Fear is a state of nervousness fit for children and not men. When man fears a creature like himself, he offends God, in whose image and likeness he is created. Man being created equal fears not man but God. To fear is to lose control of one's nerves, one's will to flutter, like a dying fowl, losing

27

consciousness, yet, alive" (2). This is what he said about Ambition: "it is the desire to go forward and improve one's condition. It is a burning flame that lights up the life of the individual and makes him see himself in another state. To be ambitious is to be great in mind and soul. To want that which is worthwhile and strive for it; To go on without looking back, reaching to that which gives satisfaction. To be humanly ambitious is to take in the world which is the province of man; to be divinely ambitious is to offend God by rivaling him in His infinite Majesty" (3). Thomas and Sarah are speechless as they take in the excitement of what their son is sharing with them.

Chapter 3

BREATH OF LIFE

Monday morning and Greg is just walking through the door at work – it is 9:30 am. As he goes through the revolving door of the office building of Hankston, Jones, and Haygan, he is still feeling the warmth of the weekend spent at Thomas and Sarah's house. He is very thankful for their friendship, despite how it started. He feels like an entirely new person. As he got to know Thomas, Sarah, and their children, he grew to love them – realizing that they are people with feelings and not animals put here to do white folk's bidding. He began to feel ashamed of what some of his friends and members of his own family had done to Black people and others that they felt were beneath them.

The incident that happened at school with his son Phillip and the Harris twins melted his heart because he loves his son with his entire being. He thinks back to how the doctors told him and Sheila that Phillip was progressing slowly in his learning ability and that he would have to be put in "special" classes. Sheila refused to believe what the doctors said and kept him in regular classes, as well as working with him at home. Phillip proved to be very bright. He was always a little small for his age, but he wasn't slow.

Greg also reflects on how the partners at the law firm reacted when he volunteered to take on the case for the Harris' - pro bono - when one of the twins broke that little boy's arm that hit Phillip. The partners did not like that. They ostracized him, calling him names like, "carpetbagger," names he had only heard in old slave movies. He did not know how to explain to Sheila why he did not get the promotion that they were both looking forward to, so he lied and took on a part-time job at a local bank doing requisitions at night to bring in extra money.

As far as Sheila was concerned, he was always working late – until he had an accident one evening due to falling asleep at the wheel. Greg told Sheila what was going on and why he did it. Sheila wanted him to quit, but he stayed, vowing that he would not let those "bigots" make him quit his job. It's been three years, and a lot of the animosity has died down. He is still not making the money that a student graduating at the top of his class should be making, but in this economy, he is not doing bad. Greg promised himself that he would stay long enough to build a client base and start his own firm.

He was becoming more and more dissatisfied with the attitudes and thought processes of his co-workers. The elderly woman that made the fatal call to the police was the grandmother of one of the partners.

Mrs. Hankston – 88 years old now, a widow living alone at the Sandy Springs Assisted Living Facility, was on a shopping excursion that the facility sponsors once a week for their seniors. That is how she came to be at that store on that fatal day of the shooting back in 2015.

Mrs. Hankston arrived in the United States from England in 1937 – she was Miriam Brightwelp then, and she was 8 years old. The South was a very different place when she first arrived in Atlanta, GA. She was not with her parents, as they did not have the proper paperwork and could not go with their daughter to the States. A male relative and his family were moving to the states on a work visa and offered to bring Miriam with them – there was only room for one more allowable person. The relative promised to take good care of Miriam.

Yes – he took very good care of her by touching her in inappropriate places when his wife was not around and threatening her not to say a word to anyone or else, he would send her back to England. Even at 8 years old, missing her parents, and being physically abused, Miriam felt she was better off in the States than how she was living in England.

She was able to complete her education, despite what was going on in the home - she put up with the abuse until she turned 17 and moved out of the relative's house. Miriam took all kinds of jobs and saved every penny she could.

At the age of 18, while working in a local library, she met and fell in love with 21-year-old Nathan Hankston, a very bright law student who told her that someday he would have his own law firm. By the time Miriam was 25 (in 1954) she was married and had her first child - Nathan Hankston, Jr.

The South in the 50s was a hotbed of racial inequality and injustices. Nathan Senior became involved with several organizations that did not believe in racial equality, especially concerning Blacks and Jewish people, or any other "non-whites." Nathan's family had a long history of owning slaves. His grandfather fought in the civil war. He proudly escorted Miriam all around Atlanta. Nathan loved Miriam's British accent and showed her off to his friends whenever he could. Nathan also loved Atlanta and beamed with pride as he took her around – showing her the different areas where the war was fought.

It was no secret that Nathan Senior was a prominent member of one of the local orders of the KKK. Miriam did not understand what the group was all about back then and would sometimes listen in on some of Nathan's conversations with his "friends" when they came to the house for meetings. It seems someone was always in need of Nathan's law expertise, and because of that, it kept him pretty busy.

True to his word, Nathan started his law firm called "The Hankston Firm" and became very wealthy as he worked on several klan-related trials. Miriam was a stay-at-home mom and was grateful that she did not have to work.

The money that she saved from her days of working went into savings, along with the fund that Nathan Senior had set up for Nathan, Jr.

As the years went by – the Hankston's did not have any other children, and Nathan, Jr. grew up, and had a family of his own, carrying on the tradition of the firm that became Hankston and Hankston. Some years later, Nathan passed the firm over to his son, Barry Nathan Hankston when he graduated from law school.

Nathan Senior died of a heart attack at the age of 70 leaving Miriam a widow at the age of 67. Miriam knew nothing of the business but was asked periodically to co-sign checks and work orders – representing her husband's part of the firm.

Not wanting to be a burden to their only son, Miriam moved into The Sandy Springs Assisted Living Facility when she turned 70 and relinquished all involvement with the law firm to her son Nathan, Jr.

The Hankston Firm was promised as a gift to Barry from his father when he passed the Bar exam. Nathan, Jr. wanted to retire early and travel with his wife Elizabeth. He made it a point to drive home the fact that once Barry graduated, he would indeed inherit the firm.

When Barry graduated, he brought on board two of his schoolmates – Clyde Jones and Matt Haygan. When Barry hired Greg on with the firm, the name changed to Hankston, Jones, and Haygan. Barry and Greg were about the same age. Barry was glad that Greg was "homegrown," a native Georgian.

He and Greg shared the same ideologies when it came to the South and what the Confederacy had stood and fought for. They both had been fed the same southern stories. Barry, knowing that Greg had graduated at the top of his class, told Greg to give it a few years at the firm and he too would eventually make partner.

Hankston, Jones, Haygan, and Carter – that sure looked good, and had a real nice ring to Greg's ears. It also would feel good to his pockets.

Unfortunately, all the hard work that Greg had put into trying to make partner did not amount to anything. Three years after that horrible incident, it was clear that Barry would never make him a partner. It was at that moment when Greg realized that he knew exactly what he needed to do.

As he started packing up his things, he felt like a ton of bricks had been lifted off of his shoulders. He had some clients but knew that he would have to basically start from scratch. He also knew that his wife wanted him to leave that firm a long time ago - he just had to get the nerve up to do it. It's going to be a little rough with Phillip about to go to college, but they will make it alright. Greg picked up his box and headed for Barry's office – yes, he felt like a newborn baby – breathing air for the very first time!

Chapter 4

THE TRUTH SHALL SET YOU FREE!

Barry sat in his office, behind his desk, with his hands folded – staring at the door as Greg happily walked out. He watched as Greg went through the office telling everyone goodbye. Barry could not for the life of himself understand how a man with a kid about to go to college would want to quit his job and start all over. Granted, he knew for himself that he would never have to go through anything like that. Growing up with everything that a child could want, and then, having a very lucrative law firm given to him. Work hard? Hardly worked at all – and he was not ashamed - in no way, shape, or form.

At this moment, he also could not understand why he was feeling just a little bit jealous. There goes a man who had to work for everything he had. There must be an appreciation for that kind of life. What about that bleeding heart for all people that he suddenly has? I thought he had learned a few things while he was working here, dam scallywag. Hell – he grew up in Georgia and should know better.

When that boy got killed a few years back it took everything in me to keep Greg from representing the family. I mean – how are you going to go against the men in blue who are here to protect US? I kept telling him that "they" were not going to win that case. My freaking grandma made the call for Christ's sake! He fought me tooth and nail about representing "them." When "their" son broke that little white boy's arm – the family wanted to put those two little chicken heads away until they were 20-years old. Thank goodness I got them to drop the charges telling them that Greg was an excellent lawyer and would see to it that their son would be put away also for bullying HIS son. Yes – I hate losing him – he is one hell of a lawyer.

"They will never be equal to us, and we God-fearing white men have to make sure of that." Barry grew up listening to comments like that from his grandfather, and all kinds of stories about how it used to be in Georgia. Stories about when the blacks knew their place and how "they" couldn't even look a white man in the face when "they" were talking to a white man, or woman for that matter. Now here we are, and a person would be surprised to know that attitudes have not changed that much here in Georgia. Yes, a lot of "them" still live here, but it is pretty much segregated as quiet as it's kept. When I go home, I can go days without seeing one of "them."

Granddad surely had some stories to tell. Barry throws his head back and laughs. I remember him telling me how the gator trappers in Florida used to take newly born black babies and put them in cages, then toss them in the water for bait. I said granddad – where did they get the babies from? Granddad would say "oh they just went into their flock of slaves and took them. Those piccaninnies were always having babies – there was plenty." Man, we would laugh.

My dad – even though he is tied in with some of the old boys here –did not go in much for some of the stuff they did with the cross burnings and all. He was not as involved as Granddad. He played his part by keeping those fools out of jail. I still have Granddad's uniform though. I keep it up in the attic. Sometimes, I put it on – hood and all. Even though I am a card-carrying member, I don't own a uniform. I'm kinda like my dad whereas I don't show up for any of the rallies. Dad told me a long time ago that we have got to stay in the background or else it could cause some damage to the firm. With all this "Black Lives Matter" crap – there are a lot of cases coming up, so I don't want to lose them on technicalities like someone finding out that I'm a "member."

As he sat there reminiscing, Barry slowly came back to the realization that he could not push it out of his mind. The jealous pang he was feeling was that he knew he never had to work for anything that he has gotten in life. His dad's name alone was the reason he was even accepted into college. I mean – who is going to turn down the son of one of the board members and top contributors to the school? He fluffed his way through and somehow passed the bar. He knew that Greg worked awfully hard, went to school on a scholarship, and graduated at the top of his class. That is an achievement that he would never experience. The other realization is that he knew that he would never have the joy of a loving family like Greg.

The thought of being with a woman made the hair on the back of Barry's neck stand to attention. For as long as he could remember, he has always had an attraction to men. He believes that his mom always knew that there was something different about him, and it was why his dad never really took up any time with him. Other than paying for his college tuition, and passing over the family's law firm, which was about all that Nathan Hankston Senior contributed to the life of his only son.

It was hard trying to keep that part of his life a secret while he was in college. Pretending to like the girls got him into the fraternity that he wanted to be a part of. It was extremely hard being in that dorm with all those guys and not being able to show how he really felt. This went on for the entire time that he spent in college. Now that he is on his own, and the CEO of his own company, he can do as he pleases - to a degree.

Barry knows that a lot of his clientele would not understand his affection for the same sex. There are several places that he can go to in Atlanta where he can enjoy himself in the manner of his choosing as long as he can pay for it. Discretion or indiscretion is the key, and Barry makes sure that the proprietor adheres to his requests for privacy.

Barry laughs to himself as he realizes that the crazy thing about his situation is that he loves black men. There is something about seeing that dark skin up against his white skin. He also loves the submission factor that is involved with his relationships.

Barry tries to justify his actions by being dominant over his love interests. He tries to ignore the frowns and disapproving looks that he imagines are on the portraits of his dad, granddad, and great granddad that line his office corridor. He has convinced himself that none of them would mind him being with a Black because of the stories they shared with him of the many slave women that great granddad had slept with. There were stories about the babies and how they were "dealt with." Well, that is the one thing that his relationships won't ever have to "deal" with.

So, no - having children is not on Barry's agenda, and he does not think that it ever will be. He does not have to pretend to like women anymore, but he also cannot afford to let everyone know about his indiscretions, so he keeps a very low profile, and practices a very secluded lifestyle. Yes – as Barry sits at his desk in his big corner office, he reflects on his life and realizes just why he is a little jealous of Greg. Freedom is not just a state of being it is also a state of mind. Barry knows the truth of the matter is that he is a prisoner of the lifestyle that he has chosen for himself.

Barry looks around, grabs his briefcase, and tells his secretary that he is leaving for the day, and to forward all his calls.

Chapter 5

WHAT'S REALLY GOING ON?

"Paging Doctor Ashley - paging Doctor Ashley. Please report to the nurse's station on 7." The hospital is very busy today, but then again - when is it not? It has been over a month now since Greg decided to leave the firm. In a way, it has been great having him home. I mean - Phillip really loves him being there when he gets out of school. Even though Phillip is about to graduate, he still enjoys his time with his dad. I am very thankful that they are close. I am also thankful that my job was able to help sustain us through this rough time with Greg not working. He is diligently trying to set up his own law firm but did not know that it would be this rough. All in all, I know that everything is going to be alright. We have some money saved up to go towards Phillip's college education, and I will work doubles if I must. I will make sure that he does not have too many financial problems as he tries to get through these college years. Wow, do I remember struggling and working odd jobs to help with my financial obligations for school. My parents could not contribute like they wanted to, and with Dad passing it made things even worse, but I made it and so will Phillip.

Sheila - are you daydreaming again? What is going on darling? Is Greg still holding it down? Sheila laughs as she looks at her friend Eric, or Ereeek as he likes to be called. Sheila became friends with Eric Lloyd Devon at once when she started working at the hospital. It did not matter to her that he was gay AND Black - she liked his spirit! He was always upbeat and that is the kind of attitude you should have when you work in a hospital. Eric is a beautiful man. I can see how men would be attracted to him. Even without makeup, his skin was flawless. He has a nice shape for a man, and as he would say - he was born a woman in a man's body. That was his running joke around here.

Eric was not the kind of gay man that flaunted his choice. He truly enjoyed his privacy and kept his love life to himself - for the most part. Except what he shares with me. I am the only one here who knows that he is in a relationship with a man that he loves.

Sheila – Sheila - Sheeeeeeeeila I have got to show you what my baby gave me last night and with that Eric throws his arm up and says, BAM! Look at this. On Eric's arm was a solid gold Rolex watch, and it was beautiful. Oh my God Eric, I have never seen one of these up close. Why in heaven's name are you wearing this here? It could get damaged or worse – stolen! Oh, Sheila, you worry too much. Why get something this beautiful and put it in a box locked away. Something like this is meant to be worn by someone like me. They both laugh. Seriously Eric - I would be a little more careful with that around here. Well Sheila, if someone wants this, they will have to cut my arm off! They both laughed again. All I have to say is that your lover must be very well off. Oh, he is not doing bad – no dahhhhhling – not at all. He is always giving me something, but you know what Sheila? I would love him even if he did not give me these things. He is like a little boy who is missing something in his life. I can't explain it but sometimes he has so much anger. Sheila looks at Eric and says, "he doesn't hit you, does he?" Oh, no girl please - that man knows better. Do not EVER forget. I may be beautiful, but I still have the power! They both started laughing again. No, but he keeps buying me things as if he is feeling sorry about something you know - he is always apologizing to me, and when I ask him why he just looks off into space and tells me to just please take the gift and enjoy it, or he'll hug me and ask me for a kiss. He is like a little child. Hell, I'm afraid to ask him what he's done. I wish I could tell you who it is Sheila, but I am sworn to secrecy so please don't feel bad.

You know I love you, and under any other circumstances, I would tell YOU of ALL people. Oh, Eric don't worry - I love you too! What are a few secrets between friends? They start laughing again.

Chapter 6

You Take the High Road and I will Take the Low Road

Thomas looks at his watch and notices that it is three o'clock already. He reaches for the phone to call his wife. Hey babe – I know it's short notice but – is it ok if I bring someone home for dinner tonight? It's Scotty – you know he doesn't get too many home-cooked meals and I keep promising to invite him over for some of your good ole cooking!! Hahahaha – yeah, I know – I'm glad you're off today too – but hey – you work for yourself so you can take off whenever you want! I know – I know - sorry babe – whatever you fix will be cool but Ummm how about some of your famous spaghetti!!!? Yessssssssss sir that's my baby! Thanks, babe – love you and see you about 7! That woman is gonna kill me – thank goodness she's taking some time off today.

Thomas and Scott have known each other ever since their days at Morehouse. Even though their studies took them in two different directions, they remained friends throughout the years. Scott majored in journalism and is now an anchor on the local news in Atlanta, "Channel 7, Metro-Atlanta News." Thomas always kids Scott about being friends with a celebrity. Scott laughs and tells Thomas – no man you're the star in the family.

Scott has been single for a long time and Thomas and Sarah are always trying to hook him up with somebody. Scott joked with Thomas when he got the invite – hey man – I know y'all ain't tryin to hook a brother up tonight are you? Thomas laughed himself because he had to admit – we do be tryin to hook him up. Especially Sarah! Hahahaha – wow some of those women she introduced him to – well – some were ok I guess – but there were a few that I was embarrassed to introduce him to. Sarah seems to think that just because the woman is nice that she will be right for Scott, but I roomed with that brother, and I kind of know the type of woman that he likes. Hell – Scott is a freak!

If I told Sarah about some of the stuff, we used to do – anyway – I better stop all this reminiscing and get out of here! Scott's car is in the shop and it won't be ready until tomorrow so I better head on out. He finished his 6 pm broadcast and told me to meet him at Farmingdale's men's store.

Scott Templeton – THE MAN! Standing in the mirror trying on the new suit that he's about to buy for the upcoming News and Documentary Emmy Awards being held this September in New York. He was trying to decide if he wanted to get a tuxedo or a suit. He finally decided on the suit. Yes - he is being nominated for the story he did on sex trafficking and how prominent it was, and still is here in the US. A lot of folks did not know or did not want to believe that it was also going on right here in the good ole South. When I uncovered the story about a gang out of Malaysia that had set up shop here, people were horrified to learn that young women were being drugged, kidnapped, and sent out of the country to be used as sex slaves. They were preying on young, homeless women. Women they thought nobody would miss. Until one day a woman came to Atlanta looking for her sister. People in the area had seen her, and someone remembered seeing a van that kept coming around. They noticed that the men inside "spoke funny." They also noticed a woman that resembled the woman in the photo that the family member was passing around had gotten into the van. People said the men were "helping" her into the van. No one paid it any mind – thinking that it was some folks trying to rehabilitate somebody – you know – get them cleaned up and off the streets. One homeless person had the good sense to get the plate number of the van.

A friend of mine on the police force shared some information about the case with me. He thought that I might be interested in doing a story on human trafficking.

He said he knew that it was going on and shared the story about this missing woman noting that the plates on the van were registered to a foreign Malaysian diplomat. That was all I needed. Why would a diplomat need a decrepit old van?

Next thing I knew – I was on a plane to Malaysia. My boss told me that I was on my own, and that the station would not be responsible if anything were to happen to me. Here I am – a Black man going to a foreign country to get information on human sex trafficking. It was hard getting anyone to talk to me. I had to pay someone to take me around and interpret conversations for me. Hell – I almost fit in – I just couldn't speak the language. I learned a few words to get by but paying that interpreter was the ticket.

At first, I was a little concerned that he would betray me but after I paid him some money upfront, he took me wherever I needed to go and got me the information that I needed.

By the time I got back to the States, I had my story. Unfortunately, the young woman that was kidnapped was never to be heard from again. That is the horror of it all. Once these women are "taken" from here or anywhere and shipped away – they are rarely ever seen again. As far as that diplomat is concerned – we couldn't touch him, and that van was also - never seen again.

After I shared my story on the show – my boss was ecstatic! I got a raise, and now I am being nominated for an award. "Yesssss - I AM THE MAN," Scott said out loud!

Hey man! Are you ready? Thomas was standing in the door watching Scott admiring himself in the mirror. Alright – alright – I'm liken that suit man. Looks like something I would buy! LOLOL – yeah right – in your dreams brotherman! What – you think I can't get that suit – boy look at this – Thomas takes out a wad of singles and starts throwing them at Scott. They both start laughing. Put your clothes on - you know I had to bribe Sarah to cook for you tonight! Not true at all – Sarah loooooves me! They continue to laugh as Scott goes into the dressing room to get dressed. I'll be ready in a sec – thanks for coming to get me – appreciate ya!

So, you're sure this is not another attempt to get me hitched!? Scotty – you should know by now that I would warn you but naw man – it's Friday and we are simply inviting you over for some of Sarah's fabulous award-winning spaghetti! Speaking of award-winning – congratulations on your nomination! We're all proud of you! Well thank you – thank you – it's about time that I get recognized for all my efforts!! Wow – how much more humble can you get hahahahaha – but hey you do deserve it! I mean – there is no way in hell that I would go to a foreign country and risk my life for a story. I would have been shittin bricks thinking that somebody was gonna rat me out! Yeah, I ain't shame to admit that I was scared but I knew there was a story, and the fact that it was linked to someone that disappeared from here made it even more interesting. I don't even know if "interesting" is the right word to use.

I was fascinated with the fact that someone would have the audacity to come into the United States and pull some shit like this. Then that sucka had the nerve to be a diplomat!! We give those folks too much leeway to come here and do whatever they please and because they are diplomats – we can't touch them. I don't even think he was sent back to his country.

That poor woman that came here looking for her sister got no satisfaction, other than the fact that someone recognized her, and saw her get into that van. That's all she knows. She has to take comfort in knowing that she was here.

Well, you helped her get some of that satisfaction by doing your story. It shed a lot of light on the fact that it is going on – even in this neck of the woods. Yeah man – people just seem to come here to Atlanta and disappear. We have all those people that came from New Orleans after the flood – I mean – they had nowhere to go.

There were people all over the place. It was a breeding ground for a sex trafficking situation. You would be even more surprised to know that a lot of Black women and children have been reported missing from here.

The numbers would scare the hell out of you. There was a time when Black women would come here just to get a shot at dancing at Magic City, remember? They would get off that Greyhound bus right across the street and go right into the club. I used to see them, man. A lot of them didn't know what they were gonna do here – all they knew was "I could make some money dancing." Hahaha yeah, dancing – right! Scotty - remember all those nights we spent in Magic City? Yeah, but T we were young – thought we were the shit cause we were Morehouse men. We had our pick of any woman we wanted Black – Brown – White – it didn't matter. Yeah, those were the days!

Now T I know you're not reminiscin' bout THOSE days!!? You got the pick man – Sarah was a fine specimen!! Hahahaha – specimen – you sound like the nutty professor Scotty –hahaha. Okay, she was perfect for me. Was? What do you mean by that T? Is everything alright with you two?

Did I say was? No man you know I love Sarah – everything is good. It's just that – things have been different since we lost Jeremiah. It's been over three years and things are just really -- different. That's the only way I can describe it.

Aah damn, T – this is the last thing I wanted to hear. Not my two-favorite people in the world. I know that what went down with Jeremiah and those cops was foul. We all felt helpless when it came to trying to get justice for what happened but – the way things have been going with Black folks and this so-called justice system – it's justice for them and just us period. It's almost like we don't have any rights.

I mean – you're successful – I'm successful -- but if we get stopped for the slightest thing, no matter how many titles we have behind our name, or how many awards we get, we are liable to become just another statistic.

Hey Scott – don't let me rain on your parade! Everything's cool man – as a matter of fact (Thomas snickers) wait until you hear what your favorite Godson is doing for his senior project! That's right wow – Jamille is graduating this year!! Time sure does fly. WE ARE GETTING OLD!!! Ohhhhhh nooooo – YOU'RE the one getting old my friend. T is doing this thing gracefully. People tell me all the time that me and Jamille look like brothers. Man, they're just tryin to soup you up – look at all those grey hairs. WHERE – hey stop playin man!

Scotty is laughing hard cause Thomas almost went off the road trying to look in the mirror at his head. Man, watch out – you got precious cargo in here. I can't believe you are still so vain! ME!? You were the one standing in the mirror talking about YESSSSSS I'M THE MAN!

Well, you weren't supposed to hear that. Anyway – tell me about Jamille's project. I think I'm gonna wait and let him tell you.

He's all excited saying he knows you of all people will understand where he's coming from cause his mother and I think he's lost his mind. Okay, okay – maybe he inherited some journalism skills from his Goddaddy! I'm gonna see what he's working with. You know you and Sarah ought to encourage him – don't tell him his idea is crazy. Oh yeah? Wait till you hear what it is – you might have to eat those words. Even for you, this might be a little out there. Then again – I'm talking to the man that risked his life in a foreign land for a story. Hell – I might have to eat my words! All jokes aside – I know where he's coming from, but he worries me Scotty – this thing is consuming him.

Brotherman – if you're not gonna tell me what it is before we get there then snap it. You over here getting me all worked up and I don't even know why. It must be something. Now I can't wait – not only for Sarah's spaghetti – but to hear this news. I know he's gonna make me proud. Shut up Scotty – I don't know if I want you to encourage him on this. T – either tell me what it is or cut it out . . . don't matter – we're here – I can hear it for myself!

Chapter 7

A CHILD SHALL LEAD THEM

As both men get out of the car, Jeremiah opens the door and runs out to greet them – hey Uncle Scott – boy am I glad to see you! Oh, and congratulations on your nomination – I've been bragging about you all around school! Sooooo, you got some brownie points dropping my name? Thomas rolls his eyes and says "whatever" very playfully sarcastic. They all laugh as they walk into the house. Sarah greets Scott with a big hug – Scotty – so glad to see you! It's been a long time. I know - well I've been begging for a meal for a while now – didn't your husband tell you? Yes, but with so much going on – hey – you know you don't need an invitation – just stop by whenever you want – *our casa is su casa*!

Oooooweeeee I love it when you speak in the language of love!!! Thomas gives Scott an exasperated look and says man that's not the language of love – French is!!! Everybody starts to laugh as they enter the living room. Hey Scott – can I get you something to drink? Yeah T – I'm a little thirsty – what you got? Well, being that it's Friday and you probably don't have anything to do tomorrow but pick up that fancy car of yours – I figure we can have a little taste – what you think? I got some rum, vodka, a little Henny – what's your poison?

Sarah shouts from the kitchen – WINE – wine is what we drink with spaghetti! The two men look at each other and quietly shake their heads as Thomas pours them both a shot of rum. Sarah yells out what? Why is it so quiet in there? Jamille starts to laugh as the guys put their hands over their lips to shhhhush him.

Hey Jamille – now what is this idea you have for your school project – I'm dying to hear about it. Sarah yells from the kitchen once again – ohhhhhhh no – not until after dinner - when everybody has had a chance to digest their food!

Awwww mom – you act like my idea is the worst thing in the world. Wow, you guys have got me all siked up – what in the world is going on? Sarah – comes out of the kitchen – Jamille – help me set the table so we can eat. You can tell Scotty all about your project after we eat – don't you want his full attention? Scotty laughs – hey I don't know about anybody else, but I'm ready to eat – let's get it on!

Thomas pushes himself away from the table holding his stomach – babe – woman you put yo foot in that sketti!!! Yeah, mom – man that was good! Scotty looked at Sarah and then looked at Thomas – I'm sorry to have to tell you this man but – I am totally in love with . . . your wife's cooking!!! Thomas throws his napkin at Scotty and Sarah tells them to get up and go into the living room while she cleans up. Oh, and by the way – Jamille – let him have it!!!!!

Jamille tells Scotty that he has to get his notebook from his room and runs upstairs. He flies down the stairs skipping steps as he stumbles into the living room. Hey man – be careful – Scott's not going anywhere – believe me – I think we all have piqued his curiosity. Ok – here it is Unc – when Jeremiah was killed, I nearly lost it. I was angry at everybody. I blamed his death on prejudiced people. It seemed like everywhere I turned Black folks were getting gunned down in the streets for whatever reason and when it happened to my brother, I felt helpless. I didn't know what to do or what I could do. I began to think – what's the use? These white folks don't want us here so why do we keep trying to be here? I got to thinking about slavery days and how we were treated. Black folks were getting lynched for looking at a white person. We got beat for the slightest thing. We weren't allowed to read, less more speak. Did you know that we weren't even allowed to laugh out loud in the presence of white folks? It seemed like nothing had changed except the WAY they killed us.

Jamille – you truly feel in your heart that nothing has changed? I mean – if nothing changed – we wouldn't be able to have this discussion in this beautiful home. I wouldn't have had the opportunity to go to school – nor you!

Unc – of course, some things have changed. Ok – I take it back. It wouldn't be fair for me to say that NOTHING has changed but when you have these deaths and no one is being held responsible for them what do you do? How am I supposed to feel? My mom even said that there are times when she is so glad to see me and dad come through the door. Trayvon Martin's mom can't say that anymore. Eric Gardner's wife and kids can't say that anymore. So, I got to thinking - what would happen if every Black person in America were to just up and leave?

Scotty looks at Thomas – Thomas looks at Scotty and shrugs his shoulders. Jamille continues. See – according to The Atlanta Black Star, an online news resource, which published a report from Nielsen that stated that from the year 2000 to 2014, the Black population's growth rate more than doubled that of the white rate of 8.2 percent AND doubled faster than the U.S. population as a whole. Jamille takes some more papers out of his bookbag - it is projected that by the year 2060, the Black population will increase from 45.7 million to 74.5 million adding up to about 17.9 percent of the U.S. population. (4)

In 2015, we reached a sort of "tipping" point as powerful media consumers, and cultural influencers across a wide range of industries – I'm taking this information from the publication – not my words! Those industries include television, music, social media, and social issues. Now unc – I don't want to bore you with a lot of statistical stuff, but I needed this for my report. I have to show the economic contributions that we make as a people to this country and what would happen if it were to suddenly be taken away!

Another piece of information is that the Nielson report that I am referring to, did their calculations based on households earning $75,000 or more per year. If those numbers represent that – what do you think we represent as people that make far less!?

54

Black buying power supposedly reached $1.2 trillion . . . Scotty interrupts – hey man supposedly is not a word – at least I don't think so. Jamille looked at Scotty – Unc come on – ok – Black buying power was said to have reached $1.2 TRILLION in 2016 and will be $1.4 trillion by 2020! That information came from Georgia's Selig Center for Economic Growth! (5) Concerning the Gross Domestic Product, that combined spending power would make Black America the 15th largest economy in the world! (6)

By this time – Sarah has joined everyone in the living room. Scotty looks at his friends and says, "I'm impressed – keep going." Jamille continues - so America's economy would definitely take a nose dive if we were all to leave! Scotty asks – and where would we go? Well – that part I haven't figured out yet but if we were to ever leave, I do have some ideas on how we would govern ourselves. It would be different than what we are doing here that's for sure!

So Jamille – where did you get this idea from and why are you entertaining it? Did Brian Kennedy put these ideas in your head? Unc – Brian Kennedy opened my eyes to a lot of our history that I never knew about. We weren't taught a fraction of the things that I learned from Mr. Kennedy. When I spent that Summer in New York with him – he gave me a history lesson that I will never forget. The things that he shared with me; I don't think I will ever find in a book anyway. Please don't get the wrong idea about Mr. Kennedy – he doesn't even know that I was gonna use this as my subject matter for my school project. He probably would not have wanted me to do it.

I look at my family and other Black families and see their struggle. Most folks are living paycheck to paycheck trying to make it. I think that it's a shame that on top of trying to make it, they have to wonder if their loved ones will make it home because some racist might decide that it's a good night for a killing!

Unc - after Jeremiah was murdered – I got to thinking – these folks don't want us here – they never did. Why do we keep trying to live with them? Thomas yells out "now see what I mean? I told you not to get too wrapped up in this crazy idea Scott – and not to encourage it." Oh, but you're wrong, T – I think this will make for a great human-interest story. Jamille – would you be willing to come on my show and talk about your senior school thesis paper?

Wow – for sure? I mean yes – yes – that would be awesome! Sarah shakes her head – oh no! We're gonna get booted out of the United States. Once this airs everyone's gonna think we're racists! Thomas looks at Jamille – son – did you think of the repercussions of what a thought like this could provoke?

Dad – it's just a hypothesis. It will also let everyone know that we DO matter. Black people spend a lot of money in this country – yet we get treated like second-class citizens. Actually dad – did you know that WHEN we were brought here (against our will) we were not ever meant to BE citizens? We were just supposed to work the land and farms to help keep the people here happy. I don't know - maybe it will open up some eyes. Sarah looks exasperated – but will it do any good? Do you think it will help to stop the violence? Or – create more?

Mom – my intentions are not to cause any trouble – I just want to open up some eyes to the fact that we as Black people do contribute to this country and that it would not be the same if we were to leave.

Scotty answers – right now sis – it's just a graduating senior's school paper – and an interesting paper – but for now – that's all it is. I'm gonna get you on Wednesday's 6 o'clock show – so when you leave school – come straight to the station.

Baby!!! Our baby is gonna be on the 6'oclock news!!! Isn't this exciting!!? Sarah – you're encouraging this too? Yes, and you should too! Freedom of speech and all that – you remember how it was when we were in college? Thomas – we both were on the debate team – come on. You used to be all over everything and everybody! Where do you think your son got all this from? Wellllll – I kinda thought he got it from his handsome and intelligent Unc over here! Thomas starts to laugh – man yeah – he got it honest – got a way with words. Ok – we'll be there!

Great!! (Scott smiles as he thinks to himself about the Emmy he will probably get from this story) Yessssssssir – this is a very interesting concept.

Chapter 8

Am I My Mother's Keeper?

Damn, I do hate coming here. The smell of Bengay mixed with rubbing alcohol makes me want to throw up. Ever since my grandmother caused that boy to get killed, she seems to have completely lost her mind. Every Friday like clockwork I come here to this sunshine factory for the elderly to sit and wait for her to utter some kind of word to me. Sometimes she acts as if she doesn't even know I'm here. Then there are times when her recall is so on point. That woman will rattle off people's names, places, and events as if what she was talking about just happened today.

I guess I can't complain too much. I mean – she put herself in here. She's paying for it herself. All I have to do is show up on Fridays. I don't know why I put myself through this. I never know who I'm going to see. Daffy knows nothing lady or Tammy total recall.

Tammy total recall relives the time of the shooting. The doctors don't know what triggers it – but it was brought on by the shock of seeing it happen and knowing that she was responsible.

58

Good afternoon Mr. Hankston! It was such a beautiful day today that one of the orderlies took your grandmother out to the garden for some fresh air. Come this way . . . I know the way thank you!

Sonny!! It's so good to see you (oh no – it's Tammy total recall). Grandmother - how are you? You are looking like one of these flowers out here - simply beautiful! This fresh air is doing you a great deal of good! Oh, I know – isn't it wonderful!! The flowers are so pretty and this morning – the birds were out singing – I love it!

You know sonny - I was thinking – we ought to do something for that poor boy's family. Grandmother - we have done all that we can do. You just need to relax here and not think about that anymore. Now, now – I'm your grandmother and I still have some say-so regarding the finances in this family. I think you ought to draft up a check to give to that family. I know that money won't bring back that poor boy, but it may help the family through this very difficult time. Grandmother - it's been three long years. Everything is all settled. There is nothing left for us to do. All of a sudden – just like that – she gets quiet and doesn't say another word.

Barry looks at his watch and notices that he has been sitting with his grandmother for over an hour without speaking. Just as he was about to get up to leave, the orderly came out saying that it was time for Mrs. Hankston's dinner, and that Barry was welcome to stay if he wanted. No thank you – I think I will just take this as my queue to leave! The orderly says she will give them time to say their goodbyes and she will be back. Barry kisses his grandmother on the forehead and tells her that he will see her next week.

As Barry walks away – Mrs. Hankston watches until he gets on the elevator. The orderly grabs the back of Mrs. Hankston's wheelchair and asks if she is ready for her dinner. Mrs. Hankston looks at the orderly and says "why yes I am starving – what are we having tonight? I hope it's spaghetti – I love spaghetti!!"

Chapter 9

CHICAGO - CHICAGO

Well, people – I bid you all fare-the-well and wish all good things for you as we approach this faaaaaboulous weekend! As Eric (pronounced Ereeeek) prepares to leave work, he is beaming at the thought of this being the first weekend in a long time that he has not had to work.

I cannot wait to get home – kick off these hospital shoes, get out of these hospital clothes, and get into a nice hot tub of water! I love baths! Ever since I was a child - my mom never had to make me take a bath!

The night nurses standing around the desk all started laughing! Hey Eric – do you like candles? One of the ladies starts to tell him about a candle she bought when he got a phone call. Karen – girl I'm out the door. Karen waves Eric off and tells him to go on and take his phone call. Karen text me the info and I'll go check them out – hello hello? I'm on my way out - hold on a sec – I will see you ladies on Monday!

I am all yours but give me time to get home and get out of these clothes. Eric has the biggest grin on his face as he is trying to talk on the phone and get to his car at the same time. Yes – I'm just happy to hear your voice and can't wait to see you! No - I can cook something – you know I can throw down in the kitchen but - - - ok – if you want to bring something make sure you add some crab cakes to the list. You know the ones from that Italian restaurant that I like. Yes – babe – ok. I'll see you around 11 tonight. Oh, and don't forget my champagne!!

Eric hurry's through the parking lot, stopping for a second to admire the beautiful Rolex watch that is on his arm. He looks at it – looks up to the sky, smiles and mouths the words "thank you Lord" – and gets in his car to head home.

Growing up on the Southside of Chicago wasn't at all fabulous, especially for someone like Eric. Having two sisters, one brother, and a dad that was so embarrassed by him - that he refused to acknowledge him as his son – even to this day. His sisters didn't help much. Eric was always very pretty for a boy. At least that's what everyone used to say. When he was growing up, his sisters would involve him in their "dress up" times. Using him as a model for their makeup and wig try ons. His mother would laugh and say how cute he was. But when he started to like putting on the makeup and wigs, it wasn't funny anymore.

Eric's dad was so embarrassed by his elder son's alternative lifestyle choice that he would look for reasons to physically abuse him. It wasn't enough that Eric suffered humiliation from his peers at school, and others in his neighborhood, but he also suffered from his dad's hatred of him. As Eric is driving, memories flooded his mind.

Eric's mother and father were introduced to each other at a party for one of their mutual friends - she is West Indian, and he is Jamaican, it was an unlikely pairing, but they soon fell in love and were married. How they ended up in Chicago he doesn't know. Eric Lloyd Devon came into this world after his two sisters and three years before his brother. His mother worked at Chicago Hospital as a nurse's aide and his dad did maintenance work wherever he could find it - taking care of a family on a maybe salary had to be hard on him.

His dad eventually landed a job with the Chicago Board of Education in their maintenance department and life was ok for a while.

The beatings started when Eric was about seven years old - his dad thought that his firstborn son was going through a phase, but when he saw that he was enjoying putting on the makeup and playing with his sister's dolls, Lloyd Devon could not have a son of his doing these things. "For Christ's sake," he would say - "he has a younger brother" - he didn't want his younger son thinking that it was ok for a boy to be doing such things and behaving in such a way. "I will not have an ante man living in my home! I will beat it out of you!"

Ante man - Eric had heard those words so many times from his dad - it is a Jamaican term meaning that he is not a fully developed man. If it were not for his mother's love - he doesn't know how he would have survived long enough to leave. His older sisters feel as if they played a major role in him being "that way." They didn't understand that I have always felt that I was born a woman in a man's body!

As Eric pulls into his driveway tears are streaming down his face. Why do I continuously do this to myself!!? I have a great job - I'm in love - I AM loved! All that hurt and pain is behind me! What is wrong with me!!? He grabs some tissue from the glove compartment - get yourself together Ereeeeek - the one who loves you is coming over and you MUST look your best for him - no red eyes and no daisy down in the dumps!

Eric wipes his eyes - puts a smile on his face, grabs his things, and heads into his home to get ready for a lovely weekend.

Chapter 10

PROMISE KEEPERS

Wednesday morning in the Harris home is nothing short of chaotic as they get ready for Jamille's appearance on the news that evening!

MOM!!! I don't want to wear a tie - DAD please help me!!!

Thomas laughs uncontrollably as he watches his wife and son debate back and forth about why he should or should not wear a tie. Seems it's been a long time since there was so much laughter in the house. Thomas reflects a little on how he almost lost his family along with the death of his son Jeremiah. Looking at the both of them, he realizes that love never dies - you just have to hold on!

Hey, you two - let's see if we can come to some kind of a compromise. Jamille - your mom wants you to look like a college professor (he snickers) while you on the other hand want to rep your age group and look cool - am I right so far?

Sarah jumps in - listen I was the captain of my debate team - don't mess with me - you are WEARING a tie young man - no compromise - no discussion! Jamille you are about to graduate from high school - the whole world will be watching you - including reps from the colleges you applied to - get the picture!?

DAD!!!? Thomas hung his head down and smiled - son - let me help you pick out a tie.

Okay, we're back in 5, 4, 3, 2, 1, And we're live! Channel 7, Metro-Atlanta T.V. News' Scott Templeton. Good evening everyone! Our story tonight centers around a senior from Walton High School. For those who do not know, the high school has a prerequisite for graduating students that require them to write a thesis paper on a subject of their choosing. I am here with Walton High School senior Jamille Harris, who, just three years ago lost his twin brother in a police-involved shooting. Jamille has chosen to write for his graduation thesis, the hypothesis of "All Black and Brown People leaving America."

In the spirit of full disclosure, I am very proud to say that Jamille is also my Godson; I call him nephew - and he calls me uncle. Hello Jamille! Hi Unc! First of all, you look very nice, and I love the tie! I also want to thank you for agreeing to be on the program! Jamille, how did you come up with the idea of basing your thesis paper on Black and Brown people leaving America?

Well, you know Unc, it was a few things. I never have gotten over my brother being murdered by the police, and then, all the police-involved killings of Black and Brown people in the news lately. It all made me start thinking ... this is crazy! Why are they treating us this way? We can't do anything. We go to the store, they kill us! We go for walks in our neighborhood, and they kill us! They say our music in our car is too loud, and they kill us. We are home in our bed, and they break in and kill us! I just got fed up and said, "Why don't we all just leave this place!?" What would they do then, if they did not have us to do all the crummy jobs that nobody else wants to do?

I then started doing some research and discovered how much we as Black people contribute to the GDP of this country. I looked at the buying power that Black people add to the economy.

According to Georgia's Selig Center for Economic Growth, Black buying power in 2016 is projected to reach $1.2 trillion and is projected to reach $1.5 trillion by 2021. (5) Regarding the Gross Domestic Product, their combined spending power would make Black America the 15th largest economy in the world! (6)

The Atlanta Black Star, which is an online news resource, published a report from Nielsen which stated that from the year 2000 to 2014, the Black population's growth rate more than doubled that of the white rate of 8.2 percent AND doubled faster than the U.S. population as a whole; it is projected that by the year 2060, the Black population will increase from 45.7 million to 74.5 million adding up to about 17.9 percent of the U.S. population. (4)

So, I hypothesized that the reason we see so many Black and Brown people being killed by police and whites, in general, is that White people see themselves quickly becoming the minority in this country. They are afraid that a majority-minority population might take control of everything and start treating them the way that they have treated us all these years.

Scott says, "hmmm interesting - okay, but if we leave, where will we go?" Jamille smiles and answers - "why - back to Africa of course!!! It's only natural that we go back home! Remember - this only became our home AFTER we were put in chains and forced to come here!"

All right my Nephew... Wheeeew!!! That is quite a topic! Very powerful! Congratulations on your graduation and keep up the good work! Thanks, Unc!

This has been Channel 7, Metro-Atlanta T.V. News' Scott Templeton in Metro-Atlanta with Walton High School senior Jamille Harris. Have a good evening!

Greg, Sheila, and their son Philip were home glued to the television, watching Jamille being interviewed by his Uncle Scott on the evening news.

Greg was blown away - WOW he did a great job! Yes, he did Sheila added. Phillip smiled clapped his hands and said, "YEAH MAN, HE NAILED IT!"

Greg, I'm a little concerned - Greg quickly stopped Sheila and looked at Phillip saying, "well let's get this celebratory dinner ready - they'll be back soon!"

Chapter 11

REALITY STEPS INTO VIEW

Scott and Jamille are laughing exuberantly as they leave the newsroom to join Thomas and Sarah.

Here he is! That's our son Babe! Thomas was beaming! Sarah gushed Oh baby you were great!! The way you handled yourself on T.V.! You looked so grown and handsome! I am very proud of you! Sarah had the biggest grin on her face. Scott hugged Sarah and grabbed Thomas's hand with a soulful grip saying, "Hey what about me?" You were good too man - everybody laughs! Come on let's go - Sheila is preparing a celebration dinner! Sarah then whispered to Thomas, "I hope this was the right decision, to let him pursue this project. You know we still have crazy fools running around with sheets on after all these years."

As soon as the words came out of her mouth, they reach the lobby, and right outside the front door, they are shocked by a massive protest that is going on outside the station. Alt-right protesters, in camouflage fatigues, with body armor and long guns, marching back and forth chanting,

"NIGGERS AND JEWS SHALL NOT REPLACE US! YOU BETTER LEAVE THIS COUNTRY; GET THE HELL OUT - ALL OF YOU!"

"Damn they didn't waste any time getting here did they!?, Scott shouted, Let's go out the side door!" As they begin to head toward the parking lot someone in the crowd yells, "there he is!!" and starts running toward them. Oh my God Sarah murmurs loudly and quickly takes off her shoes so she can run! As they're running, they hear a loud horn - BEEEEP, BEEEEEP! A black chauffeur-driven limousine pulls in front of them with the horn honking blaringly loud! The driver yells to all of them - come on, get in! Thomas looked at Scott, do you know him? No, I don't know him, do you? I've never seen him before. Jamille said, "Me either!" Sarah grabbed Jamille and looked at Thomas as if to say - I told you so!

Scott's news nose gets the better of him - Okay, it's all right, you're with me. We'll get our cars later! I won't let anything happen to you all! Come on, let's see what he wants with us. They jumped into the car and it speeds away from the curb, and the rowdy crowd outside the T.V. station.

Once inside the limo, they are greeted by a familiar face. Hello everyone, my name is Barry Nathan Hankston, senior partner of the Hankston, Jones, and Haygan Law Firm. Immediately, Thomas says "we know who you are"! The question is – why are you here and what do you want from us? Barry attempts to dismiss Thomas' disdain for him and proceeded to explain. Your son Jamille, I must say, his thesis has generated a lot of interest from a lot of different people. Jamille sheepishly responds - I guess…, but I didn't give it to anyone but my teacher at school. I don't know how anyone else even knew about it.

I think I can help you understand, typically when the Walton High School senior class submits their senior thesis papers for graduation, they are usually sent to a team of leading members of the Atlanta Business community for evaluation. I must say, when the team read your thesis paper, they were extremely impressed. Yours received the highest scores from all the team members. There are prominent individuals around the country that would like to explore this idea with you further.

They believe that you may have the perfect solution to a growing concern in this nation. They believe this may also be the way that this country escapes another civil war.

Thomas blurts out - civil war!!? Man, what is this nonsense you're talking about? Sarah screams – why are you bothering us? You're the son of the woman that called the police on MY son and you now want to have a conversation!!?

Jamille screams out - whaaat!!? - let us out of here - there's nothing we want from you! Scott's newsy nose is once again taking all of this in - he leans in looking from Thomas to Barry - then he says - "I'm interested in what he is getting at - Thomas - Sarah - let me find out what this is all about!

Barry apologizes profusely for everything that happened and lets them know that his mother has never gotten over the unfortunate incident and is in a nursing home facility as a result of it - her mind comes and goes.

Well, my son is gone, and he is not coming back!! Sarah screams out of her tears. What more do you want from us!!? At that moment - after about a half-hour of driving around, the limousine drives up to Scott's car in the T.V. station's parking lot. By now, the protesters are gone just as quickly as they had assembled. The chauffeur opens the door for everyone as they exit the car. Jamille, here is my card - as he begins to hand it to Jamille, Thomas quickly grabs it from his hand. Anything you need to talk to my son about, you can talk to me!

Yes - yes Sir Mr. Harris - I can explain everything to you if you will please give me a call when you are ready to sit down with us and talk about putting real meat on the bones of this subject.

Scott promises that he will find out what Barry Hankston was talking about and let he and Sarah know something as soon as he can. He assured them that he would protect Jamille at all cost.

With that – they all got in their cars and headed to Greg and Sheila's house. No one was in the mood for a celebratory dinner, but they also did not want to let them down by not showing up.

Chapter 12

THE CHOSEN ONE

Phillip opens up the door and immediately senses that something is wrong. Thomas and Sarah enter the house with Jamille following. Phillip asks, "what's going on?" We saw the interview and it was great, what happened!? Thomas says, "I guess you didn't see the news?" Greg and Sheila come out of the kitchen looking at everyone - hey what's going on? Again, Thomas says, "I guess you all didn't see the news?" Sarah was still crying - Sheila goes over to Sarah - what's wrong honey? What happened!?

Thomas lets them know what happened outside the station and also told them about the conversation with Barry Hankston in the limousine. It seems that some government officials want to speak with Jamille about his thesis. They mentioned something about possibly stopping a Civil War! I don't know what the hell they're talking about. Scott is going to come with me and sit down with Barry Hankston to find out what this is all about.

Greg says, "Barry Hankston, My ex-boss?" Sarah screams out YES YES that's the same Hankston! Sheila says, "oh my God is this nightmare ever going to end!!?" I'm so sorry Sarah I'm so very sorry that you all have to keep reliving this nightmare! Sarah turns to Thomas and yells out, "I told you this was not going to be a good idea now I'm afraid for our son - what could they possibly want with him!!?"

Greg is listening intently and tells Thomas that he will be going also because they will need some kind of legal representation at that meeting no matter what happens.

All the while they were discussing the issue - Scott was on the phone with the network chief explaining why he left the station without getting the story on the activists that were protesting outside the station. He could be heard yelling that Jamille is his Godson and he had to get him out of there.

Greg turns the TV back on and there is breaking news about Jamille and the interview.

Scott tells the network head that he will call him back and tells everyone to be quiet for a moment - everyone begins to listen just in time to hear a reporter talking to one of the protesters - he is telling the reporter, "if that nigger wants to leave, we want him and anyone else that wants to go with him to go and get the hell out of here!! We don't want you here!" The reporter tells the protester that he will not tolerate that kind of talk! The other protesters start to rally behind the one that is talking - agreeing with everything he is saying.

Now there is a group of Black people starting to gather around - they are shouting that they are ready to go, - "YALL never wanted us here no way - pay me reparations for my slave labor - then I will be ready to leave." The reporter is beginning to get nervous because the crowds are getting larger. You can see police activity starting to develop.

A protester shouts, "if you want a race war you got it - we're ready!" Someone from the group of Black people shouts out, "yeah that's exactly what you want you violent ass muthafuckas- you don't know how to live and let live - you always want to go to war!! Yeah, we will gladly get the hell out of here!" The reporter must have gotten a queue from the station to wrap it up - we will keep you informed of further developments this is ... Greg turns the TV off.

Scott speaks first, "Jamille you have awakened the beast!" Jamille, looking confused says, "all I wanted to do was to propose a hypothetical situation - I don't want to cause any trouble." Thomas sat down near Sarah - they looked at each other with a what are we gonna do now expression. Son don't worry, we're gonna get this straightened out somehow.

Greg asks Scott if he knows when he will be meeting with Barry Hankston. I'm going to call him right now - my network head keeps blowing up my phone, but I don't want to talk to him right now - all he's interested in is the story. Thomas snaps back at Scott, "well what about you? What's your interest in this man!? Isn't this the reason you even wanted Jamille on your show!? You knew this was gonna start some shit!"

Scott puts his hand on Thomas's shoulder, "hey man - that's not fair - I admit that as a newsman I saw a great human-interest story and that the story was a little risky but I never in a million years thought it would stir up the racial pot! For whatever it's worth - I think it's time, and Jamille appears to be the chosen one."

Chapter 13

REVELATIONS

The next day, Thomas is getting ready to go to work and Jamille is getting ready for school - the Harris family is trying to have some semblance of normalcy until they hear a lot of commotion outside their home. "Now what!?," Thomas says as he peeks out the window.

There are news cameras along with a group of Black people congregating outside their home. Thomas tells Jamille to stay in his room as he and Sarah go downstairs to find out what's going on.

As Thomas opens the door, he is bombarded with questions - "how can we sign up to go? - where will we live? - what will it cost?" - the news reporter asks Thomas and Sarah how they feel about their son starting a revolution and shoves a mic in Thomas's face. Thomas screams, "what are you people doing here!? What do you mean revolution!?" The crowd is starting to get bigger as someone shouts out that they saw the interview and is ready to go now! The news reporter explains to Thomas and Sarah that they have been getting phone calls from people wanting to know how they can sign up to go. Thomas yells, "GO WHERE!? Our son was just asking a hypothetical question"- Sarah jumps in, "it was for his senior thesis paper - he didn't mean it literally!"

The news reporter tells them that a delegate from Ghana has contacted them and will be doing an interview this morning to officially offer an invitation to all Black and Brown people to come live in their country and it all stems from your son's appearance on Scott Templeton's news segment the other day. How do you feel about that? Can we speak with Jamille? Sarah shouts, "no you may not!! Thomas, please make these people go away!"

Thomas tells everyone to please leave the premises - they have nothing further to say - he takes Sarah and goes back into the house. Thomas also tells Jamille that he is to stay home today. Thomas gives Scott a call telling him what is going on outside his home.

Chapter 14

THE MEETING

Thomas, along with Scott and Greg, pull into the parking lot of the Hankston, Jones, and Haygan law firm. They sit there for a moment to discuss the situation. Thomas speaks first - you know he mentioned something about preventing a civil war - what could he possibly be talking about? Scott jumps in - not sure but I have to tell you that the phones in the newsroom have been blowing up! You got Black folks wanting to know when they can leave and if there is somewhere to go. Then you got White folks - half are saying good riddance and half want to know what's going on and why is this happening! It's like the circus has come to town. Greg says - for all it's worth - we don't want you to go anywhere - we meaning me, Sheila and Phillip - I was told vehemently by those two to straighten this nonsense out!

Jamille was a nervous wreck last night, and Sarah couldn't sleep because people kept riding by the house yelling and shouting! Someone even threw eggs at the house - poor Sarah thought they were gun shots - she jumped up and ran to Jamille's room to see if he was ok. I feel helpless because I can't put my hands on anyone - I don't mean hands on literally- I mean - I can't pinpoint whose doing what - they ride by so fast and we don't know if they WILL start shooting at some point - I feel like I can't protect my family. I haven't ever felt like this - it's a strange thing but - I was thinking - this must have been what it felt like back in slavery days when a Black man could not protect his family - even when he could put a face and a name to his aggressors - he couldn't do anything.

Scott puts his head down - then looks at Thomas and Greg - I swear I didn't mean for any of this to happen! As we sit here - do you know that a representative from Ghana is at the station doing an interview to make an invitation to all Black and Brown people to leave the US and move there!?

Greg says "oh my God!! What is happening!?" Has everyone lost their minds!? I'm not going to pretend that I know how you are feeling or that I totally understand how you are feeling, but I do know that I use to be one of those people wishing that Black people or ANYBODY that wasn't white would all go to hell - I'm ashamed of ever feeling that way - I'm ashamed that my family was a part of all that - I'm ashamed that my race instigated this whole mess - my God - I'm starting to feel like I'm responsible for all of this! Thomas I'm so sorry man! Thomas puts his hand on Greg's arm saying, "it's ok man it's not your fault!"

Scott yells for everybody to stop talking!! What are you doing!? - you are friends - you've been friends for years!!

Before we all start singing *kum ba yah* let's get the hell out of this car - go into this building and find out what this man has to say! Greg says, "hold on, before we go up there, I have something else to tell you. You both know that I use to work for Barry, right? You also need to know that Barry is very high up in the ranks of the Klan. Really high. I don't know what he has to say but my gut tells me that it's not going to be good." Scott says, "how high?" Greg paused for a moment - looks at Greg and Thomas and says, "he's a Grand Wizard." As they get out the car Thomas moans, "Aww man, what have we gotten ourselves into?"

Inside the building, the desk clerk greets them saying, "Mr. Harris and party? Mr. Hankston is expecting you, please - come this way." The clerk takes them through a door where there is an elevator waiting. The clerk ushers them onto the elevator, pushes a button and walks away as the door closes. They are all quiet as the elevator reaches its destination. The elevator door opens up to a big room, and Barry is standing there to greet them. Good morning gentlemen! He shakes everyone's hand. Greg - it's been a while hasn't it? It's good to see you!

Thomas looks at Barry saying, "if you don't mind - please tell us what this is all about!" Yes - yes - Barry leads them to the table in the middle of the room - please have a seat! Greg says, "I thought this was going to be a meeting of some sort - with other people." Barry goes on to explain that they will be meeting with his clients virtually, and as he said that a monitor lowers itself behind Barry's head. A voice speaks - good morning Mr. Harris, Mr. Templeton, and Mr. Carter - thank you all for agreeing to meet with us.

Scott says, "us!? We don't see anybody but Barry - what is this? Some kind of joke!?" Please be patient Mr. Templeton. We will be having a Zoom meeting shortly. We have members of the Congressional Black Caucus joining us and we have members of the President's cabinet who will also be joining our meeting. There will also be a delegation of Black clergy in attendance, along with representatives from the Guyana government.

After several hours of back and forth amongst the meeting participants, it was found that the parties involved did not take the idea of Black and Brown people leaving the United States too lightly. Everyone in attendance at the meeting was in total agreement, that there has been a number of unfortunate situations that left a lot to be desired as to Black and Brown people living peaceful and prosperous lives here in America.

There was discussion of a possible reparation payment on the table. Thomas looked from Greg to Scott – is this really happening!? All of this is taking place because of a senior in high school? I mean – this is too much to comprehend! Everyone was quiet as Thomas spoke. 400 years of abuse – countless numbers of lives lost - years and years of just trying to be treated fairly, and this is what it took!? I DON'T BELIEVE YOU PEOPLE!!!!

Someone from the Black clergy spoke – saying that God does not work on our time – he does things in his own time and we should not question his actions. For whatever reason – THIS is the time that he has chosen for all this to take place, and your son was the catalyst! Thomas – Mr. Harris, please accept that now is the time! Let us not be weary nor negligent in recognizing this opportunity for us all to have a chance for a better life!

Thomas yells out "BUT I WAS BORN HERE"! WHY DO I HAVE TO LEAVE!? The voice in the monitor answered Thomas as best he could, saying that this is why we are all here right now – yes you were born here – we all were born here, but were we ever welcome here!? We have a chance Mr. Harris, to have the life that our ancestors wanted for us – don't you want that for your children and grandchildren?

At that comment – Thomas looked at Greg and Scott and began to cry. The voice in the monitor gasped – Mr. Harris I am so sorry – I do apologize – my condolences on the loss of your son – we all feel your pain, which is why you should want even more to be on board with this great opportunity!! We have two governments here at the table willing to finally DO SOMETHING about the atrocities that were done to us – we are talking reparations AND a place to call home!

It was agreed that it would take place within five to ten years. A lot of planning will go into bringing this all to fruition.

After it seemed an eternity in that room, at that table with a monitor hanging over their heads, the men in that room listened as they finally reached an agreement on reparations to be paid to the descendants of slaves brought to America in the 1600s until human trafficking was officially ended in the 1800s.

The government agreed to compensate black people for the 40 acres and a mule which it had initially agreed to during the period known as "Reconstruction" until it was reneged upon in 1877. A reparations payout amount was decided upon that is owed to some 40 million+ black people. This negotiated settlement which would amount to more than 10 Trillion dollars would be used to persuade them to leave America. As black people board ships to leave, each person would receive a reparation payment of $250,000. Although it was understood that this payment was meager considering the abundant wealth that slave labor had enabled the United States to amass, becoming the greatest, most prosperous nation on earth. Upon accepting this offer of reparation, the recipient must leave and never return to America – under any circumstances.

As Thomas, Greg and Scott leave the meeting, they are all speechless as to what they have just witnessed and was so much a part of. Scott was sworn to secrecy as they work out all the necessary rudiments of putting this most aggressive ideology in place. Because Scott is a news reporter, he had to sign a non-disclosure agreement – they all had to sign one. This was too big of a story to get leaked out before everything was put into place. To make matters worse, Jamille's graduation was coming up. Thomas looked straight ahead – he didn't know what to say. Greg kept saying unbelievable. Nevertheless, it was a very quiet ride back to the Harris house.

When they got to the house, Sarah was there waiting with Sheila – Jamille and Phillip had not gotten home from school yet. Sarah immediately asked what had happened. Thomas told them both to sit down as he and his two friends, regardless of what they promised not to disclose, tried to explain what they had just been a party to.

Chapter 15

THE GRADUATE

The month of June, to Sarah, has always been just the perfect time for a graduation. She always thought that ever since she was a child. She would see the seniors looking so very grown up and ready for the world. It would seem to be forever sunny and bright. It was that way when she graduated from high school and, also when she graduated from college. Now here she is, getting ready to see her son march across a stage tomorrow to get his high school diploma. Sarah quietly began to cry as she sat on the side of the tub. She did not want Thomas to hear her sobbing as she thought of their other son, who did not live to see this day. Sarah dips her towel in the water that she has run in the tub and slowly wipes her face. A smile makes its way across her face because she knows in her heart that Jeremiah is smiling down on his brother today.

Through the bathroom door, she can hear Thomas talking to Jamille about life and what he may or may not be looking forward to in the future. She could hear him telling him how proud he and his mother are of him and his choice to major in political science. They instinctively knew that their son would aspire to a political career.

Sheila and Greg are in the kitchen, sitting at the table. Greg puts his hand on Sheila's – they are so proud that their son is graduating tomorrow with honors. Counselors would tell them so many times when Phillip was growing up that he was slow. Sheila never believed that about her son, she always had faith in him, and she knew without a doubt that her son was smart as a whip. Phillip comes in the kitchen and sees his parents sitting there looking at him with tears in their eyes – awwww mom, dad – why are you guys looking so sad!? Tomorrow is going to be a great day, and before it gets too crazy around here with family and friends, I want to tell you both how much I love you, and that I thank you for being the best parents that a big head boy like me could ever have!! As he reaches out to hug them, they both grab him and he yells out – mom – dad – I can't breathe!!!!

The night sky is filled with stars – both sets of parents are sitting outside on the steps of the Harris' home contemplating the joy of the big day. Jamille and Phillip went out with some friends saying that they would not be out too late. Greg spoke first – we raised two good boys didn't we? Thomas chimed in – yeah we did! Not sure what its going to be like for them five or ten years from now. Sarah said please Thomas, let's not spoil anything by thinking about that right now. Sheila looked at Sarah – but how can we not think about it or talk about it – its real and already put in motion – oh my God – what kind of world will this be? Why does things have to change so much and so drastically? Sarah – let's promise right here and right now to always remain friends, kind and loving towards one another – you are like my sister!!! Thomas says Greg – I have a question to ask you – if – I mean when it is time for us to go, and you have a chance to stay or leave, what will you do? Greg shakes his head – no I'm not answering that – it's not a fair question Thomas because the option is not offered to me. Persistently Thomas says - but if you had the option, what would you choose. Honestly? Greg said without hesitation, me and my family would be in a cabin right next to yours!

Thomas takes out an envelope – I want to share something with you both. He looks at Sarah as she gives him the nod to go on and tell them. I received a phone call the other day from a lawyer for Mrs. Hankston – she is the lady that called the police that day. Well, he told me that Mrs. Hankston left her entire estate to Jamille. You see – for the last few years after the loss of Jeremiah, we have been getting these checks sent to our bank account with a note that said "for Jamille's college fund" – large amounts of money – we didn't know where they were coming from, we figured some goodhearted person just felt terrible about Jamille losing his twin brother and wanted to help with his college. Well as it turns out, it was Mrs. Hankston all along. All these years she was riddled with such guilt that she bankrolled Jamille's entire college tuition to any school he wanted to go to. Sadly, she passed away this morning from natural causes, and we received the call with the information about her estate. We haven't told Jamille yet – I mean, how do you tell a young boy that he is suddenly very rich!?

Greg – we are going to need your help as her son Barry is trying to fight us on this – although I was assured by her lawyer that there is nothing that Barry can do, as she was in her right mind when she signed the papers, it seems that she pretended to have dementia so that Barry would leave her alone, she knew that he didn't want to be bothered with her. The assisted living facility that she lived in were all people that she hired to take care of her, unbeknownst to Barry.

Greg and Sheila were ecstatic – oh my God – what are you going to do with all that money!!!? Maybe you don't have to leave now!!? Greg started laughing – I bet Barry is fit to be tied right now. Serves him right! Well we have a lot to celebrate on tomorrow, and I can't wait to see Jamille's face when you tell him – wow – hey can we borrow a dollar!!? Greg throws his head back and laughs so hard he almost falls off the steps. All jokes aside – we are very happy for Jamille but we must remember the type of man that we are dealing with here in Barry – need to watch out, keep a good eye on him – don't know what he may try and do, especially with his affiliations.

The next day, both households were filled with family and friends as everyone was getting ready to head to the high school for the graduation. Jamille and Phillip snuck out of their houses and met in the backyard to congratulate each other privately.

Phillip told Jamille that he was so lucky to have a friend, a brother like him and that they will always be brothers for life – he then put out his hand to shake Jamille's hand but Jamille looked at Phillip and said – hey what is this!? We hug in this family so you might as well get ready cause Imma hug you – ok – here it comes! They both start laughing as they hugged each other – then waved at each other as they left the backyard to leave with their families for the graduation.

Sitting in the auditorium, Thomas and Sarah, and Greg and Sheila sat next to each other – the ladies were holding hands as they watched their sons get their diplomas. Thomas and Greg were ready with the tissues, it was kind of synchronized as they gave the ladies their tissues to wipe their eyes, almost comical. It was also bittersweet, as nobody but Sarah could see Jeremiah walking side by side with Jamille up to the podium when they called his name. She secretly said "congratulations to you both"!

Chapter 16

WHEN THE CHICKENS COME HOME TO ROOST

A number of years has gone by since that fateful meeting regarding paying reparations to Black and Brown people here in the United States so that they can leave and never return, and to think that I, Barry Hankston played a tremendous role in the initiation of it!

I don't know why it is taking so long for this to happen, everything is in place, the Guyana government is ready for these porch monkeys to come home – what is the problem!?

Ever since that old woman died and left her entire estate to that boy it has been a nightmare here. I have been trying to find some way to reverse that decision. How could she do that to me!!?? I took care of her all those years and this is how she repays me! It's alright though – I do have a plan and believe you me – they are not leaving here with my money, that's for sure! I don't know how in the hell that boy had the nerve to run for office. He's not gonna be here that long to run anything. My God, how far does the sympathy trail go? He has been riding on the coattail of his brother's death for much too long. Now he's a congressman of some sort – a young, rich congressman at that – spending my money! Oh yes Mr. Congressman – you will pay, and I will get my money back and all that belongs to me!

Chapter 17

WHO KNEW WHY THE
BLACK MAN SANG

Thirty-five thousand feet in the air, the 7 AM Delta flight out of Hartsfield Jackson International Airport in Atlanta was on schedule for a 9:30 AM arrival at Reagan International Airport, in Washington D.C. The wealthy freshman Congressman, Jamille Harris stared out at the slow dawning of a new day from his window seat, his mind leisurely drifted to thoughts of his long-departed twin brother, Jeremiah, and his more recently departed father, Thomas who at the age of 51, suddenly died of a heart attack. It's been ten years since his high school graduation, and a lot has happened.

A sheepish smile breaks through his gloom despite the tears in his eyes as he imagined what his brother would think of him graduating from Morehouse College, Law school, and then becoming the Congressman from Atlanta's 2ND Congressional District. I think Jeremiah would be proud of me, and Dad too, he thought to himself. I decided a long time ago, that I was not going to let my brother's death be in vain. I was determined then, as I am now that I am going to make some good come from the senseless taking of his life.

One of Jamille's committee assignments in congress is on the Department of Homeland Security Council. As such, his committee is meeting today with Ghana's Minister of Tourism, Arts, and Culture Mrs. Barbara Oteng-Gyasi. She is here to re-state her country's "Year of Return" initiative which was launched on behalf of African Leaders all across the Africa continent by Ghanaian President Nana Akufo-Addo" in Washington, DC last year.

Jamille felt excited by the happenings on the African continent, it's just as he had envisioned in his high school thesis paper 10 years ago. God, I miss my brother, Jeremiah. I also miss my Dad not being there to see me sworn in as a United States Congressman, a Black Moses telling Pharaoh, "let my people go." The thought causes a smile to swell up inside of him.

Jamille settles back into the warm, succulent, leather back seat of the waiting limousine on this cold, blustery February morning in Washington D.C. He takes out his cellphone and calls his mother, as he promised he would as soon as he arrived in D.C. Hi Mom! I made it to DC safely and wanted to give you a call! Oh, hello baby! I am so glad you had a safe flight. I know you have a big meeting today, but don't forget to call me later to let me know how everything went, okay? Okay Mom, I will, I love you! I love you too son!

After his call, Jamille reclined comfortably back in his seat and enjoyed a hot cup of coffee as the limousine crossed the Potomac River and rounded the National Mall past the Lincoln Memorial and the Washington Monument as it made its way toward the United States Capitol building.

Good Morning, Mr. Chairman, Ladies and Gentlemen of the Congress of the United States of America. On behalf of Ghanaian President Nana Akufo-Addo, and all the leaders of the other African nations, greetings.

From Africa we have noticed that racism here in America continues to be a deadly pandemic, for which for more than 400 years now, our brothers and sisters in the United States of America have yearned for a cure.

We continue to open our arms and invite all our brothers and sisters home. Ghana is your home. Africa is your home. We have our arms wide open ready to welcome you home. Please take advantage, come home build a life in Ghana, or any of the other nations of Africa, you do not have to stay where you are not wanted forever, you have a choice and Africa is waiting for you. (7)

From abroad, it appears to us that the sentiment of this nation is nothing but resentment toward black and brown people. Racial unrest continues to bubble to the surface more and more. Numerous incidences of police shootings and killings of young black and brown people in what should be routine traffic stops. But in every case, the killings are determined to be justified use of deadly force. These cases keep piling up across this country. No one in the black and brown communities are immune to being gunned down by hate groups or law enforcement officers without any repercussions.

In this country, it appears to be open season on black people. People are in the streets in massive demonstrations, demanding accountability for the senseless killings of unarmed people of color. They are screaming, "Black Lives Matter" to no avail. We see on our televisions, thousands of your people flooding the streets in major cities disrupting traffic, accomplishing nothing. Again, I appeal to you, you do not have to stay where you are not wanted, you have a choice and Africa is waiting for you.

I have been authorized to tell you this amazing news. A summit of all the leaders of the African nations was held in Nairobi, Kenya, the ancestral homeland of the father of your first black President of the United States of America, Barak Obama.

The nations of Africa had grown weary of the lawlessness and corruption that had plagued many of their countries since their independence from colonial rule.

They were also fed up with being taken advantage of by more developed nations that ravaged the natural resources of the continent. The leaders of Africa finally realized that their collective resources of the continent would vastly exceed the natural resources of all the other nations of the world combined.

At the African Summit as it became known, the leaders agreed to the unification of the entire continent into a Republic that will be called The United Nations of Africa. The capitol of this new government will be in Nairobi, Kenya. All disparate military forces across the continent are being reconstituted into one military. A force to be reckoned with that will be second to none. The constitution of these United Nations of Africa will be modeled after the unrealized constitution of the United States of America with three branches of government: Executive, Legislative and Judicial.

The formation of this new United Nations of Africa (UNA) is an opportunity to come to the aid of Black people the world over who live in nations such as yours that do not respect them. They are routinely discriminated against, persecuted, and relegated to live in slums. They are subjected to inferior educational systems designed to support White privilege and keep minorities as second-class citizens.

Against this backdrop, the new United Nations of Africa is making appeals to Black people the world over to return home to Africa. Come home to your motherland where you will be welcomed, respected, and well-compensated as never before for your contributions to making the United Nations of Africa the greatest nation on earth. Most importantly, ladies and gentlemen, I have also been authorized to inquire whether your Congressman Mr. Jamille Harris would consider accepting an offer on behalf of our newly formed United Nations of Africa, to be the new nations' first President.

Chapter 18

ON THAT GREAT GETTIN UP MORNING

Finally, the long-awaited day had arrived. Aboard his private yacht, that he named JEREMIAH, in honor of his deceased brother, Jamille and his mother, Sarah finished settling into their adjoining staterooms. They both came out onto the balcony of the ship to watch as The Royal Caribbean International Cruise Line, The Oasis of the Seas, docked at pier 105 in Miami, Florida, began its journey along with over 6,700 passengers. Everyone waving and saying their goodbyes to their White friends, neighbors, and former co-workers, and to America, too.

This same scenario was being played out on twenty other cruise ships, all along the several piers dotting the Miami coastline and every other seacoast across America. Hundreds of cruise ships filled to capacity were leased by the Federal government to transport Black and Brown people to the African continent. The airlines were also employed in this mass undertaking, sanctioned by the US government to get all the Black and Brown people who wanted to leave, safely out of the country to their destination in Africa.

Throughout America, a sense of euphoria, jubilation, and festival exuded hate groups such as the Alt-Right, Neo-Nazi, Proud Boys, and KKK, to name just a few. These groups had long hoped that this day, or a revolution would one day come to rid themselves of their so-called, "Nigger" problems.

Members of these hate groups would not have missed this day to save their lives. They literally, lined the piers yelling expletives and screaming for joy. Some of them threw rotten tomatoes at the people on the balconies of the ships. "Get the hell out of here, you bastards! Don't ever come back," they shouted.

Sarah wept as she listened to the vulgar insults, and obscenities screamed at them as the ships left port headed for the open seas. Mom, it's all right, God is with us! I don't believe that he brought us this far to leave us.

Chapter 19

Parting Is Such Sweet Sorrow

"Huh, huh, huh, Aah...," Barry sighs as he rolls off Eric and onto his side of the bed. "Yeah, babe, oooooh that was good! I worked up a little sweat whew! Eric gets up and sits on the side of the bed looking lovingly at Barry - honey, I have something to tell you. I've been thinking, and I decided that I'm going to take the government's offer of $200,000 to leave the country.

Whoa, whoa... what are you talking about? After all, I've done for you. You're gonna just up and leave me like that. What the hell? Are you seeing someone else? Nooo, Barry, please - I'm not seeing anybody but you. Then why do you want to leave!? Why would you do this to me, Eric? You know how much I love you?!

I just don't want to be the only Black man, a Gay one at that, left in America when everyone else leaves. Honey, you understand, don't you?

"You ungrateful bastard," Barry says as he rolls out of bed. After all I've done for you! Why - you wouldn't have even gotten that job at the hospital if it weren't for me! $200,000 - he goes to his safe and takes out stacks of money. If that's all you want, here - take it! Eric looks at the money then looks at Barry - sweetie it's not just the money - like everyone's been saying - it's time. I know you love me, but Black and Brown people have never really been welcomed here. Can you please try to understand? As much as we love one another, we can't even let anybody know that we're together. I've been sneaking around with you for years - baby - I'm tired of doing that - of living like this. I'm also tired of all the senseless killings of my Black brothers and sisters. Every single day there's another tragedy. I'm surprised that Black folks stayed here THIS long!

All the while Eric is talking - Barry has slowly gone over to his dresser - opens the drawer and takes out a gun. Eric has his back to Barry. He suddenly turns around and says, "babe why don't you come with me!?" Just as he says it Barry pulls the trigger! As Eric is lying there in a pool of blood, Barry stands over him - you know - to me - you're just another nigger like all the rest. Eric is now crying and pleading with Barry to please get him to a hospital. Please Barry I don't want to die! Barry, in a fit of rage tells Eric to shut the hell up - he puts the gun point-blank to Eric's head, and pulls the trigger again! Blood splatters all over the bed and the wall, the lifeless body of Eric slumps down on the bed in a puddle of blood.

Barry sits down at his desk - opens the drawer and takes out a notebook that has a lock on it - he gets a key out of a different drawer - opens the book and dials a number. Yes - a cleanup is needed - you will also need to take the body down to the Okefenokee swamp and get rid of it. The door will be unlocked.

Chapter 20

Smooth Sailing from Now On

Unbeknownst to many people, and, all too many black and brown people in particular, is the fact that The Thirteenth Amendment of the U.S. Constitution does not entirely eliminate slavery. Section 1 states, "Neither slavery nor involuntary servitude, *except as a punishment for crime whereof the party shall have been duly convicted, shall exist within the United States, or any place subject to their jurisdiction." (8)

Nationwide, prisons and jails discharged their incarcerated Black and Brown people onto buses that were used to convey them directly to waiting cruise ships. The prison industrial complex industry came into being as a result of a "poison pill" clause (see above underlined) inserted into The Thirteenth Amendment. Once someone is convicted of a felony, they are striped of many rights typically afforded ordinary citizens such as: the right to vote, the ability to get a good job, the ability to get a college student loan. This ploy has been used for decades to maintain the status quo of an inferior class of individuals to help prop up the false claim of white supremacy.

Several corporations benefit from this thinly veiled scheme to perpetuate slave labor in America through a program of mass incarceration. Those large corporations use prison labor to produce some of the products that they sell. The inmates they employ typically earn between 90 cents to $4 a day. (9) Thus, orange became the new black. This is the reason for the policy of over policing of black and brown communities.

Truth be told, it is easy to claim supremacy over a group of people that you go out of your way to deny them their right to vote, and enact laws and policies designed to keep them down. However, through all the obstacles laid before them, blacks continually excel and overcome situations and circumstances and prosper in the arenas of: Politics, Medicine, Entertainment, Business, Science, Engineering, Architecture, Technology, and Education.

Major metropolitan cities across America virtually emptied themselves of their populations of Black and Brown people. Urban areas throughout the nation were seemingly deserted. The American population was greatly diminished.

Immigration laws designed to deter Black and Brown people from America were succeeding more than anyone ever imagined they would.

Businessmen and farmers began clamoring for the government to pass new legislation to somehow reverse the trend of these people leaving America. Not unlike the Israelites who ransacked the Egyptians during their exodus, Blacks through reparation payments of more than $10 trillion had all but depleted the Federal government's coffers. As a result, Congress passed emergency legislation to increase taxes on the remaining populous to fund essential government services.

*underlining added by the author for emphasis

Chapter 21

Steady As She Goes

The cruise ships have all been several days at sea traveling at the top speed of 24.5 knots per hour. Newly named President of The United Nations of Africa, Jamille Harris and his mother Sarah's transatlantic voyage to Africa of 5,174 nautical miles will take them 9-days of sailing. In the meanwhile, they spend their time enjoying the peaceful waters while reclining on the veranda outside their staterooms.

Across the horizon, one could see the other cruise ships of their unescorted convoy. So far so good, up to now there had been smooth sailing, no rough seas.

That evening, Jamille found his mother alone on the balcony outside her compartment. "Mom, why are you out here alone? You could have rung my room and I would have come out here with you. "Oh no I'm all right, I was just enjoying the sweet smell in the air, and the cool breeze off the ocean. I was looking at all those beautiful stars in the sky and thinking about your father, wishing he were here.

She let out a deep sigh, we had always talked about taking a cruise like this, but never got around to doing it. I think he would have loved this view.

A hundred nautical miles off the coast of Saint Maarten, passengers noticed several naval vessels off in the distance, trailing them. Before long, some passengers who had previous military experience identified the ships as destroyers. They had just been off in the distance, but now they had quickly made up a lot of ground fast and were rapidly closing in on the convoy.

The Captain became concerned after perusing them more closely through his binoculars. He noticed that they were flying Alt-Right colors. The captain got on the radio and raised the Coast Guard to request aid. "Coast Guard Station San Juan, Puerto Rico. This is Captain Maris Jamison of the Royal Caribbean International Cruise Line, Oasis of the Seas cruise ship.

We are currently about a hundred nautical miles east of St. Maarten. Requesting U.S. Coast Guard help as we are being stalked by several naval vessels flying Neo-Nazi insignia, over. I believe they are pirates, over."

"Royal Caribbean International Cruise Line, Oasis of the Seas. This is Chief Petty Officer, Jerome Masters, Coast Guard Station, San Juan, Puerto Rico. I am sorry Sir; the U.S. Coast Guard has no authority in international waters to protect your flotilla. Your request has been relayed to U.S. Naval vessels operating in the area, over."

Passengers on the other ships in the convoy also noticed the approaching vessels and became nervous and afraid when they saw the Nazi insignia they were flying. Who are these people and what do they want with us? What are we going to do?

White supremacists, Alt-Right, Klansmen, and other hate groups for years had been creating a navy of their own consisting of decommissioned U.S. Naval vessels: Destroyers, Cruisers, and a Submarine. They had a total of seven vessels piloted by their members who had prior military experience. These groups came together and devised a scheme to sabotage the program of black and brown people leaving America to go to Africa.

Under the command of the Grand Dragon of the Atlanta branch of the Ku Klux Klan, Barry Hankston. They planned to sink one or more of the cruise ships in international waters and force the rest of them to return to America. These were pirates, plain and simple, who viewed themselves as patriots. They intended to rob the passengers of their money and possessions, then bring them back to America as twenty-first-century slaves.

Then, as if to confirm everyone's worst fears, the pirates fired a torpedo and struck one of the cruise ships! There were three very loud blasts, Boom! Boom! Boom! Torpedoes struck the ship twice causing collateral damage and other onboard explosions. Jamille heard over the Captain's radio on his yacht, "fire in the engine room!" Passengers could be heard screaming and yelling, Oh MY GOD! The sounds reverberated in the pitch black of the night. All the ship's bells sounded, DING! DING! DING! Captains were shouting commands over loudspeakers to crew members, "Launch the lifeboats!"

Jamille heard an SOS from another one of the sister ships, "Mayday! Mayday, this is the Royal Caribbean International Cruise Line, Harmony of the Seas Cruise ship. Mayday! Mayday this is the Royal Caribbean International Cruise Line, Harmony of the Seas cruise ship. We are 100 nautical miles off the coast of St. Maarten! We are under attack by pirates! We have taken two torpedo hits! We are beginning to sink! We have lifeboats in the water and are abandoning ship! Then we heard the sound of automatic weapons, TA TA TA TA TA TA TA TA TA TA TA! The pirates were shooting the people in the lifeboats. Again, we heard explosions ringing out, BOOM! BOOM! BOOM! Another ship was hit. The night sky lit up as bright as noonday from the flames of the three burning cruise ships. Sharks began a feeding frenzy as some passengers dove off sinking cruise ships into the water. The howling, screaming, and wailing of women and children was almost unbearable.

Then suddenly, the waters began simmering, bubbling over … the waters began stirring, more and more, and the bubbles grew. A mile, or so in the rear of the convoy, the waters looked as if it was a sloshing, boiling cauldron, incessantly bubbling. Fearfully, passengers jumped back away from the ship's railings and braced their backs against the exterior walls along the veranda, "What is this," they shrieked.

Just below the surface of the water, something could be seen rising up out of the ocean. A wall of water spewing upwards into the air created a wall of separation between the convoy and the pirate's flotilla. WHOOSH! WHOOSH! WHOOSH! Submarines! They were submarines, several of them surfacing behind the convoy. Jamille and Sarah watched in amazement as they arrayed themselves, facing off against the pirate flotilla. The submarines had an insignia on their ships that represented The United Nations of Africa! The pirates fired torpedoes at the submarines. The sub commanders gave commands to their respected crews to launch anti-torpedo missiles into the water. These missiles intercepted, exploded the advancing torpedoes, and eliminated the threat they posed before they could reach their targets. Then the submarines proceeded to engage the pirate ships full-on in the firefight. They retaliated with a massive barrage of Tomahawk Cruise missiles fired at the pirates. SWISH! SWISH! SWISH! Followed by explosions, BOOM BOOM BOOM BOOM BOOM BOOM and 50 caliber machine gun fire, TA TA TA TA TA TA TA! SWISH! BOOM! Again, and again the onslaught of Tomahawk Cruise missiles persisted, SWISH! SWISH! SWISH! BOOM BOOM BOOM BOOM BOOM from the submarines toward the pirates. Then, the RA DA TA TA TA TA TA TA sound of 50 caliber machine gun fire. The firefight continued on into the wee hours… But by early dawn, a dead silence fell over the entire ocean except for the continuing rescue operations. Dead silence… Calm…

Jamille! Jamille, where are you!? I heard my mom screaming my name. Mom! Mom! Here I am Mom; it's all right! I had one of the stewards to take mom back to her room, but they could not keep her there for long – she ran and hugged me so tight that I could hardly breathe!

Then I heard someone else calling me. I am thinking to myself, who the hell is this calling me? . . . President

Harris! President Jamille Harris! Yes, yes that's me! Who are you? Mr. President, I am Captain Cedric Palmer of the South African Navy. I have orders out of headquarters in Johannesburg to safely escort your convoy the rest of the way into Cape Town.

Later that day, Barry Hankston and a few of his men were recovered from the wreckage of their pirate flotilla. They were found clinging to debris floating in the ocean. They were taken into custody by the South African Navy crewmen. Barry and his men were then transported to the International Court of Justice for war crimes at the Hague in the Netherlands charged with crimes against humanity, the murder of 352 people, terrorist attacks on three cruise ships, and piracy on the high seas.

Chapter 22

A LONG TIME COMING

A clarion call had gone out to all downtrodden people of color the world over, "Come to Africa and find peace, prosperity and rest for your tired souls." As a result, black and brown people heeded the call and began arriving to Africa in droves.

Overnight, it seemed that the African continent had been transformed into an ultramodern new civilization, the likes of which the world had never seen. Super trains traversed the continent at lighting speeds. African engineers developed commercial airplanes that generated its fuel from hydrogen in the atmosphere and released condensate as its exhaust, thus they emitted no air pollution.

This kind of technology was also implored in the production of electric vehicles that were affordable for the masses. However, there was little to no traffic to speak of as most people preferred mass-transportation over driving themselves, that was both convenient and available, day or night. These systems were computerized autonomous vehicles. "Wakanda" come to life!

Colleges and universities throughout the continent produced the most sought-after graduates, Business leaders, Doctors, and Scientists. African institutional leaders were world renown and highly recruited to teach at prestigious colleges and universities in other nations.

African scientists revolutionized the field of medicine. The philosophy of managed care which only treated the symptoms of diseases was replaced by a philosophy of managed health.

Managed health, as opposed to managed care, supplanted the mindset of so-called modern medicine which saw surgery as the key to achieving good health.

The idea of surgery, when you think about it, is quite barbaric. The idea that surgery could ever be the solution to any, and all ailments was seen as ludicrous. This antiquated mindset was replaced with the concept of restoring the body to its normal healthy state through good nutrition and holistic medicine rather than by hacking it to pieces. African scientists discovered that diseased organs could be brought back to good health, and vigor with natural remedies. Good nutrition and exercise combined with natural herbs, vitamins, and minerals could heal the body of all sorts of cancers, heart diseases, kidney problems, and the like.

This new way of supplying health care reduced the need for transplants, chemotherapy, dialysis treatments and a host of other antiquated remedies.

Revolutionary new Dental care procedures reduced the need to extract teeth. People could possibly live their entire lives with their natural teeth in good health.

As a result, the paradigms of the Hospital, Pharmaceutical, and Insurance industries were dramatically turned upside down, changed from the once money-grubbing institutions of a bygone era of greed. Now hospitals, had become simply places where people came to be rejuvenated when they let themselves get too rundown.

President Jamille Harris in his first state of the union address to a joint session of the Congress of the United Nations of Africa ... My fellow Africans, we hold these truths to be self-evident that all men are created equal, that they are endowed by their Creator with certain unalienable Rights, that among these are Life, Liberty, and the pursuit of Happiness... (10) Free at last! Free at last! Thank God Almighty, we are free at last! (11) The whole congress rose to their feet with a thunderous round of applause that seemed to go on endlessly.

Chapter 23

BE CAREFUL WHAT
YOU ASK FOR

Immediately, The United States of America felt the absence of its African American community. Stocks tumbled, leaving the US in a state of constant emergency. The monies used to fund the mass exodus nearly crashed the Federal Reserve. The entertainment industry was not the same. Sports changed drastically.

However, not every African American left, but those who stayed behind were hardly enough to help save the economy. Of course, jobs were in abundance – as there was a lot to do, but there were not enough people available to handle all the work that had to be done. The government was desperately trying to devise ways to bring people back to the States.

There were so many empty and abandoned homes and apartment complexes that it brought about largescale campaigns to entice returns, such as – offering anyone that wanted to return the proverbial 40 acres and a mule! If you came back, you would get a home with bedrooms for everyone in the family plus an extra room for guests, you would get a vehicle for everyone in the home that had a license to drive, and a guaranteed job with a competitive salary!

The federal government promised to live up to the creeds of its Bill of Rights and the Constitution which it had neglected to do in the past that included true justice for all, and it would no longer tolerate anyone to be judged by, or because of the color of their skin ever again. The government was in trouble and they knew it. The borders were once again in the news. The military had a significant loss of personnel, therefore, it could not maintain its far flung bases around the world. As a result, they also could not fulfill its obligations to its allies.

America struggled for many years, not able to regain their status in the world market, they were no longer recognized as the superpower that they once were.

Chapter 24

HELLO – IT'S ME!

Twelve years later, Jamille, his wife (Bishara, daughter of the Governor of Kenya), and their two children Jeremiah (9-years old), and Asilia (8-years old) traveled to America on vacation and to visit friends.

The United States of America's Secret Service, State, and local police escorted the United Nations of Africa's Presidential motorcade as it left Hartsfield Jackson Atlanta International Airport and went ahead onto highway 85 North to 75 Northwest to Cobb county in Atlanta, Georgia. The Presidential motorcade stretched more than a mile long, with their red and blue lights flashing and sirens blaring. Metro-Atlanta Police stopped traffic in every direction to allow the motorcade unimpeded roadway access.

Soon they arrived at the home of Greg and Sheila Carter on the outskirts of Metro Atlanta, in Cobb county. Jamille and his entourage exited their limousine and walked up the walkway to the front door when just then, the door opened and Philip and his wife, Carol, and their two children came out to meet them. Jamille, oh my God, is it really you? He and Jamille embraced one another. How are you, "Jamille, my brother?" I am fine, my brother Philip!" I'm sorry I didn't call you first, but I didn't know if I was going to have time to stop by to see you. Then I said, "I will make the time to see my brother, Philip." It has been such a long time, wow, said Jamille. I see that you kept the family home! It sure is great seeing the old neighborhood!

Jamille, how is your mother, Sarah? Well, my mother passed away 5-years ago. What about your parents, Greg and Sheila, how are they? My parents have also passed away, but all is well. Please meet my wife Carol, and this is our son and daughter Michael and Denise. Jamille beams - Hello eveyone! Hello, sir! Philip and Carol, this is my wife Bishara. This is our son, Jeremiah, and our daughter, Asilia. The children bow a native greeting to their new friends and family. Michael and Denise invite the children to their backyard – Jamille can hear Jeremiah yell out HA YAH!!!" as Asilia does a roundhouse kick over Jeremiah's head. Showing off his skills, he ducks and grabs Asilia's leg. Ahahahahaha…this brings back fond memories, Jeremiah and I used to go at it just like that. Jamille smiles and sighs…

What are you doing these days Philip? Well, I took over dad's firm when he passed. We are in the downtown Atlanta office building that used to be Hankston, Jones, and Haygan. I guess you know all about him by now, but he turned out to be a Grand Dragon of the Ku Klux Klan, and he also led the flotilla of pirates that sank two of the cruise ships that were part of your group leaving here going to Africa. The last thing I heard of Barry was that he was arrested and extradited to a prison in the Netherlands. Jamille nodded his head in agreement – yes – yes - how unfortunate for him.

Yeah, he and his gang were given life sentences for crimes against humanity and murder. Maaaan – I also found out that Barry was attracted to men – he had a lover – the guy used to work with my mom at the hospital and get this – HE WAS BLACK! His name was Eric, and he was a male nurse. Eric went missing and to this day, people are saying that Barry might have killed him – no one has ever found the body! His family says he did not leave with them and no one has heard or seen from him in years! Anyway, with that being said, all Barry's possessions in this country were confiscated by the Federal government and sold at auction. So, my firm was able to pick up his office building for a song.

Phillip looked at Jamille with tears in his eyes – I have missed you man! Well Phillip - you could have come for a visit – I am the President you know!! You and your family are welcome to come any time you like!!! They both start laughing – you know you are right – my brother The President!!! Isn't that something? It seemed they laughed and talked for hours before one of the aides knocked on the door to let President Harris know that it was time to go. This momentary familiarity was interrupted by his new reality.

The two families hugged each other with promises to see each other again very soon!

Jamille's next visit was with his Uncle (God Father), Scott Templeton, who lives in Brookhaven on the outskirts of Atlanta. As President Jamille's motorcade traveled Southeast on 75 to 285 East, Atlanta's beautiful, majestic skyline could be seen off in the distance. With its towering skyscrapers, Atlanta (the Emerald City), is truly a testament to black achievement in the heart of the Confederacy. Jamille couldn't help but think about how Atlanta started out being a Black mecca for African Americans. The motorcade slowly snaked through the affluent Dunwoody community on Glenridge Connector NE to Dunwoody Road NE until finally, it arrived at Brookhaven. The motorcade drove up a long circular driveway leading to the main house. Jamille had called ahead, so Scott and his wife, Clarice were outside waiting for his arrival. My favorite nephew, Jamille! yelled Scott. Hahahahaha! How are you son? How old are you now? Hi Unc! Jamille smiles - I am just old enough haha - I am doing fine Unc. Let me introduce you to my family, my wife Bishara. This is our son, Jerimiah (9-years old), and Asilia (8-years old). Unc, it looks like you have done very well for yourself, what's going on? I am still baffled as to why you did not want to leave!

The craziest thing you could ever imagine is that when almost all of us left here in the great diaspora to Africa. Suddenly, the Federal Government realized the error of its ways and purged all the remaining vestiges of racism. They finally made good on the promises of equal rights and opportunities for all.

Before I knew what was happening, the owner of the network where I worked was introducing me to his daughter, hahahahahaha. We fell in love with each other and got married. My father-in-law died and left the station to me. Can you believe it? Hahahahahaha, and here I am! What do you think nephew? Looking good, Unc … but isn't it ironic, that we all had to leave America before they realized how much we really needed each other?

THE END

List of Citations

1) Cover page; Quote from Martin Luther King Jr.'s speech entitled: *The Promised Land*

2) Pages 27 & 28; 2014, June 28; Philosophy and Opinions of Marcus Mosiah Garvey: *Fear*

3) Page 28; 2014, June 28; Philosophy and Opinions of Marcus Mosiah Garvey: *Ambition*

4) Pages 54 & 67; Black Population's Growth Rate; african-american-consumer-untold-story-sept-2015.pdf (nielsen.com), page 3

5) Pages 55 & 67; Black Buying Power; UGA report: Minority groups driving U.S. economy - UGA Today

6) Pages 56 & 67; Black America: 15th Largest Economy; What If Black America Were a Country? - The Atlantic

7) Page 94; CNN; June 17, 2020: Ghana Has Message for African Americans: Come Home; Ghana has a message for African Americans: Come home (cnn.com)

8) Page 102; The Constitution of the United States, Amendment 13, Section 1; Thirteenth Amendment Section 1 | Constitution Annotated | Congress.gov | Library of Congress

9) Page 102; Companies that use prison labor; <u>8 Major Companies That Use Prison Labor To Make Their Products (urbangyal.com)</u>

10) Page 113; Preamble to the U.S. Declaration of Independence 1776; National Archives

11) Page 113; Quote from Martin Luther King Jr.'s speech entitled: *I Have A Dream*